Frugal
MEDITERRANEAN
COOKING

Easy, AFFORDABLE RECIPES
FOR LIFELONG HEALTH

MELANIE LIONELLO

Founder of
From My Little Kitchen

PAGE STREET
PUBLISHING CO.

PAGE STREET
PUBLISHING CO.

FOR MY LOVE, ISAAC

Contents

INTRODUCTION

Mediterranean food has long been touted as one of the world's healthiest ways of eating. It is rich in good-for-you fats found in extra virgin olive oil, nuts and seeds; encourages a high consumption of vegetables and fruit; utilizes legumes and pulses in place of meat for everyday dishes; and highlights seafood and fish as the animal protein of choice. While the Mediterranean diet is one of the best for supporting cardiovascular and heart health, with its abundant inclusions of healthier-for-you ingredients, I can promise you that it's also one of the most delicious, enchanting, satisfying and utterly gorgeous cuisines in the world.

The Mediterranean coastline envelops the Mediterranean Sea and stretches around the south of Europe and to the west of Asia and the north of Africa. This is not only a vast area of land but also a vast range of countries, cultures and cuisines. The traditional Mediterranean diet speaks to the food and cooking practices of the people in Crete, Greece's mainland and islands and Italy. However, in this book, I will show you how to use the pillars of the traditional Mediterranean diet and elevate them using herbs, spices and specialty ingredients from all over the Mediterranean. And better yet, I will show you how to do it all on a budget.

This book is not intended to be a prescriptive diet or a sermon about what you should eat. (Although I will absolutely insist you make and eat my Garlic Bread Panzanella [page 12]!) My goal was to take my love of the Mediterranean and my travels throughout the region and weave them into my expertise as a nutritionist while taking a frugal approach (on your wallet, but not on flavor, I can assure you!). It might seem like this way of eating is expensive—I mean, it does sound pretty extravagant if you don't normally pick up these items on your weekly shop—but once you have a base pantry set up with some staple herbs, spices, seasonings and extra virgin olive oil, you'll be set to spend around $3.00 or less per serving for every single recipe in this book. Not bad for wholesome AND delicious, is it?

Having an Italian background, I have been eating and loving Mediterranean food my entire life. This has obviously heavily influenced both my palate and my style of cooking. My grandparents immigrated to Australia in the 1960s. Without knowing English and lacking money, it was important to cook recipes that cost as little as possible. And luckily, many of the dishes that are synonymous with Italy today were originally peasant dishes. Sixty years later and my nonna still cooks these meals as often as ever. Every time I visit them, my nonna whips up an amazing meal that she assures me is terrible . . . but is always amazing. I know how much joy she gets from cooking for others, and this is something that has shaped the way I cook and the hospitality I show my friends and family. As a child, and even now, I loved going to my grandparents' house and helping pick fresh vegetables from the garden. I learned recipes from my nonna, some of which I have included in this book. They are not only cheap and good for you, but also incredibly flavorful and an utter joy to eat. These recipes hold a special place in my heart.

Both my heritage and my travels throughout the Mediterranean shaped my career. I knew I had an undying love of good food, and I also realized that what you eat can profoundly impact the way you feel. This idea lead me to university to become a qualified nutritionist. I then continued studying and undertook my Honors year to research and prepare my thesis on Turkish culinary culture. Turkish cooking has always piqued my interest, with my family being from Venice and Venice once upon a time falling within the Ottoman Empire. Toward the end of my university journey, I began food blogging as a creative outlet. I shared recipes and posted images on Instagram. My following quickly grew, and before long, I got to create my very own soup to be sold in major supermarkets throughout Australia. I jumped at the chance, and the rest is history! Since then I've been posting on my blog and Instagram—From My Little Kitchen—running cooking workshops, presenting on national television and traveling the world filming all things food, which I feel very lucky to have been able to do.

Last year, I decided I would travel as much as I could, eat as much as I could and learn as much as I could. And while some of my trips weren't to the Mediterranean, they were valuable to me nonetheless. I learned how the same staple ingredients could be transformed so brilliantly into spectacular and mouthwatering dishes so different from one another. Then I hopscotched through the western coastline of Italy, over to Spain and down and around Portugal. Although these countries are so close together, they felt worlds apart to me. But the love of and use of olive oil was a thread that bound them, as well as the rest of the Mediterranean, together.

For me, Spanish food is food for entertaining. Big, robust flavors and, much like Italian *aperitivo*, the start of dinner begins hours earlier with tapas and a drink. Our favorite thing to do in Barcelona was to taste all the flavors that Spain had to offer through these tapas and *pintxos*, which are little bites of bread with a variety of toppings. One of my favorites was a pintxos topped with a slice of potato and onion tortilla. This inspired my delicious and ridiculously simple Caramelized Onion and Potato Spanish Tortilla (page 23).

Before eating my weight in *pastel de nata* in Portugal, my experience with Portuguese cuisine was minimal. But once I arrived, that all changed. I sampled incredible green wine, Portuguese black sausage and, most memorable of all, charred octopus dressed in nothing more than olive oil, lemon and fresh herbs then cooked over charcoal. My Barbecued Octopus (page 85) was inspired by that seaside meal. I use the fresh, vibrant, seasonal ingredients of the Mediterranean to bring this dish into your home.

A few years ago, while still at university, I traveled to Istanbul, Turkey, with my now husband, Isaac, to visit some friends who were living there. While I was out exploring, the fragrances floating out onto the street from the grand bazaar pulled me inside, and what I discovered was a feast for the senses. Enormous golden plates piled high and perfect cone-like shapes of vibrantly colored spices. The spice mixes I sampled were deliciously salty, but also acidic and sweet, earthy and nutty and piquant and bold. They were also subtle and mild, floral and perfumed. The food was so savory and aromatic, and I instantly fell in love . . . so much so that upon returning home, I began a yearlong research project. The topic? Turkish culinary culture. This trip inspired so many recipes in this book, from my Whole Stuffed Pumpkin with Walnuts, Golden Raisins and Herbs (page 20) and Red Lentil Soup (page 69) to Smoky Stuffed Peppers with Lamb (page 108).

Fast forward a few years and that research project propelled me to many trips back to the Mediterranean to not only learn the basics, but also to learn the art of making yogurt and cheese as well as the three pillars of ancient Greek cuisine: figs, olives and grapes. These three pillars shaped the entire diet of the wider Mediterranean from ancient times right through until today.

Slowly, I realized that I no longer cooked any other way. And even though I grew up in an Italian family, I had never eaten so much olive oil or so many vegetables. It never felt boring and never tasted bland, even if I ate the same thing over and over. The dishes I cooked for my friends and family were always swooned over, and I was always rattling off the recipe to them so they could recreate it at home. The feedback was always the same: "This is amazing!" and "It's so easy to make!"

In this book, you will find a collection of fast, simple and affordable recipes focusing on the food groups of a Mediterranean-inspired diet. These recipes can be enjoyed at any time of the day and can be paired up and made together for a family meal or a dinner party. The flavors and ingredients overlap throughout the book, which not only makes it easy to choose something for dinner but also minimizes your need to buy dozens of ingredients for just one or two dishes.

I also wanted to show you how easy cooking Mediterranean-inspired food can be, no matter how inexperienced you are in the kitchen. Creating delicious wholesome recipes doesn't have to be hard, stressful or overwhelming. You'll find that once you start cooking this way, it's just so easy. You use olive oil as your permanent base and build flavor with fresh herbs and spices, and then add body with vegetables, legumes, whole grains, seafood, poultry and even a little red meat.

A quick note: All recipes in this book use US measurements, with metric measurements in parenthesis, to make it easy and fuss-free for readers from around the world to make these dishes.

This is my favorite way of cooking and eating, inspired by my heritage, my studies and my travels. Fast, fresh and frugal. I hope you enjoy the recipes, and, as always, happy cooking!

Hearty
WHOLESOME VEGETABLES:
THE KIND YOU WILL LOVE TO COOK AND EAT

When people think of the Mediterranean, they naturally think of the sea. I do too, which is why it's often so surprising to learn that most Mediterranean-style recipes are actually built around vegetables, not seafood.

If you've ever visited anywhere along the Mediterranean coast (lucky you!), you've probably noticed restaurants, trattorias and seaside street stalls all selling delicious morsels like freshly grilled zucchini, tabbouleh and shepherd's salad, or fire-roasted peppers, panzanella and Greek briami. All of them full to the brim with flavor and vegetables.

So, when planning a Mediterranean recipe, whether its roots are in Italy, Greece, Turkey or somewhere else along the coast, it's more than likely going to start with a few key vegetables: onions, garlic or tomatoes and a generous drizzle of extra virgin olive oil. It's a humble beginning, but most Mediterranean cooking starts there, which is also why it's so affordable. Cooking primarily with vegetables and other ingredients that are in-season and available fresh from your local market or grocer keeps your shopping list cost-effective and ever evolving. If you can't find spinach, try chard. If broad beans (fava beans) aren't quite ready yet, pick up some peas. And if potatoes are cheaper than pumpkin, swap it!

In this chapter, I'll show you how simple yet utterly spectacular cooking with vegetables can be. From Whole Stuffed Pumpkin with Walnuts, Golden Raisins and Herbs (page 20) to crispy Fennel Gratinati (page 27) to Roasted Carrots with Honey and Za'atar (page 24), I want you to be so inspired by the flavors and ingredients in these recipes that you want to make them time and time again and they become your go-to recipes. And more than anything, I want to show you the flavors I grew up with—the ones I learned about during my studies and travels to this gorgeous part of the world—to really bring the joy and the vibrance of vegetables from my little kitchen to yours.

GARLIC BREAD PANZANELLA

Panzanella is a traditional Italian recipe originating in Tuscany. Its name comes from the joining of *pane*, meaning "bread," and *zanella*, which is a kind of cooking pan. The key to a panzanella salad is using old bread to make crispy, crunchy croutons. I've jazzed up this traditional recipe by adding a few extra low-cost ingredients that take it to the next level. This is a favorite to serve when we have friends over, because it makes a large bowl and is just so filling and satisfying with ripe bursting tomatoes, salty-sweet garlic bread chunks, a generous lacing of sticky caramelized onions and luscious pieces of mild and creamy mozzarella. Once you start making this, it'll never come off your rotation.

COST PER SERVING: $1.64 | YIELD: 6 SERVINGS

FOR THE CARAMELIZED ONIONS

2½ tbsp (40 ml) extra virgin olive oil

2 yellow (brown) onions, peeled and very finely sliced

½ tsp salt

4 tsp (20 ml) balsamic vinegar

2 tbsp (25 g) brown sugar

FOR THE GARLIC BREAD CROUTONS

6–8 slices (200 g) pane di casa, ciabatta or sourdough bread

⅓ cup (80 ml) extra virgin olive oil

3 tbsp (10 g) finely chopped parsley

3 cloves garlic, minced

½ tsp salt

FOR THE DRESSING

2½ tbsp (40 ml) red wine vinegar

¼ cup (60 ml) extra virgin olive oil

Salt and cracked black pepper, to taste

FOR SERVING

1 lb (500 g) cherry tomatoes, halved

½ cup (95 g) pitted kalamata olives

15 large basil leaves

1 (7-oz [198-g]) mozzarella ball, torn

Preheat the oven to 350°F (180°C).

To make the caramelized onions, add the olive oil, onions and salt to a skillet over low heat. Let the onions slowly cook for about 30 minutes until they are softened but not browning or crisping. I know it'll be really tough not to turn that heat up, but trust me, it's worth it! After 30 minutes, add the vinegar and brown sugar and cook for 10 to 15 minutes. You can turn the heat up a little at this point if you feel it needs it. Your onions should be sweet, salty and very soft.

While the onions are cooking, make the croutons. Place the bread on a baking sheet. Combine the olive oil, parsley, garlic and salt in a small bowl. Generously brush this mixture onto each slice of bread, tipping any excess onto the slices as well. Bake for 15 to 20 minutes, or until the bread is very golden. Let the bread cool before slicing into cubes.

To make the dressing, combine the red wine vinegar, olive oil, salt and pepper in a small bowl. Arrange the tomatoes in a serving dish with the olives. Sprinkle the basil and mozzarella over the top. Add the caramelized onions and croutons, and spoon the dressing over the salad.

SUMMER TOMATO SALAD

No one serves tomatoes like they do on the Mediterranean. The warm, bright summer sun grows the most stunning tomatoes that are bursting full of flavor. I love how meaty Mediterranean tomatoes are too. They are so hearty and substantial that they are often served as a meal on their own, with some bread alongside. Last year, we sailed out to Capri, which is where this salad originates and is called *insalata caprese,* meaning "salad in the manner of Capri." While Capri in peak tourist season is not the most affordable place I've ever been, this salad—using locally grown tomatoes and basil and a ball of handmade mozzarella—came in as one of the least expensive menu items. We ate the dish with plenty of fresh crusty bread to mop up the leftover olive oil and vinegar while sipping on a carafe of white wine . . . all while spending far, far less than we would on takeout at home.

COST PER SERVING: $1.55 | YIELD: 4 SERVINGS

8 red or mixed tomatoes

1 (7-oz [198-g]) mozzarella ball, torn

1 cup (20 g) tightly packed basil leaves

⅓ cup (60 g) pitted olives, any variety

2½ tbsp (40 ml) balsamic vinegar

¼ cup (60 ml) extra virgin olive oil

Salt and cracked black pepper, to taste

Roughly chop the tomatoes into pieces, removing and discarding the cores. Place the tomatoes onto a plate and top with the torn pieces of mozzarella. Place the basil leaves, olives, vinegar and oil in a small food processor, and pulse until roughly combined and the olives are still a little chunky. Season with salt and pepper. Spoon the olive mixture over the salad and serve.

ROASTED BEET SALAD WITH FETA AND WALNUTS

Beets and feta are one of the greatest flavor combinations. They work perfectly together, and a small amount of feta goes a long way. This is a great recipe that really highlights the key pillars of the Mediterranean diet: plenty of veggies, a bunch of nuts and a little dairy, all wrapped together with a hint of fruit and olive oil. I added grapes to this classic recipe for a pop of sweetness, and you could always roast the grapes (á la Roasted Grape Bruschetta [page 45]) for the last few minutes with the beets.

COST PER SERVING: $1.57 | YIELD: 4-6 SERVINGS

FOR THE BEETS

5 beets

¼ cup (60 ml) extra virgin olive oil

1 small bunch of red seedless grapes

⅔ cup (100 g) feta cheese

2 tbsp (11 g) torn mint leaves

3 tbsp (10 g) chopped parsley

1 cup (125 g) walnuts

FOR THE DRESSING

¼ cup (60 ml) extra virgin olive oil

2½ tbsp (40 ml) red wine vinegar

Salt and cracked black pepper, to taste

Preheat the oven to 350°F (180°C).

To make the beets, cut the leaves off the beets (save them for Three Greens Pesto [page 122]) and scrub the beets clean in a sink of water. Rinse the beets, then place them into a heavy saucepan and drizzle them with the olive oil. Bake for up to 1 hour, checking at 45 minutes to see if they are tender and cooked through by gently poking a skewer into one. If not quite done, put them back into the oven and check them again in 5-minute increments until they are ready. Let the beets cool until you can handle them, and carefully peel the skins off. I find a paring knife really helps here. Quarter the beets and arrange them in a serving dish.

Pluck the grapes off their stems and sprinkle them over the beets. Crumble the feta over the beets, and sprinkle the mint and parsley. Add the walnuts.

To make the dressing, combine the olive oil, vinegar, salt and pepper in a small bowl, and pour over the salad to dress it. Adjust the salt and pepper to taste and serve.

PISELLI (BRAISED PEAS IN TOMATO)

I absolutely loathed peas growing up. They tasted completely average to me, and I would complain every time they were served. Then my nonna made *piselli*, which translates exactly as "peas" (an incredibly inventive name). She absolutely won me over by cooking frozen peas in tomato with not much more than garlic and onion. I like adding a little pancetta because I love finding those firm little chewy pieces in between bites of peas, but it isn't necessary for a delicious dish if you don't have it.

COST PER SERVING: $0.91 | YIELD: 4 SERVINGS

3 tbsp + 1 tsp (50 ml) extra virgin olive oil

2 oz (60 g) pancetta, diced (about 1 thick slice) (optional)

3 cloves garlic, roughly chopped

1 yellow (brown) onion, peeled and diced

1 (14-oz [400-g]) can crushed tomatoes

⅓ cup (80 ml) dry white wine

½ tsp salt, plus more to taste

¼ tsp cracked black pepper, plus more to taste

3¾ cups (500 g) frozen baby peas

Parsley, to garnish

In a heavy saucepan, heat the olive oil over low heat, then add the pancetta (if using), garlic and onion. Sauté until the onion is soft and the pancetta is brown.

Add the crushed tomatoes, wine, salt and pepper and cook, stirring for 5 minutes. Add the peas and stir to combine. Place a lid on the saucepan and simmer on low for at least 1 to 2 hours. You will know it's done when the peas are soft and a dull green color, and the sauce will be really quite thick. Stir occasionally and adjust the seasoning as needed to taste. Serve alone or as a sauce over al dente pasta garnished with parsley, if desired.

WHOLE STUFFED PUMPKIN WITH WALNUTS, GOLDEN RAISINS AND HERBS

This is the side to make for your next dinner party. It's very straightforward and so impressive to serve: a whole pumpkin, filled to the brim with gorgeous, tender fragrant rice, with the stalk perched on top. It is soft yet firm enough to slice entire pieces out of it like a cake. You can use whatever variety of pumpkin that is most affordable for you. I generally find Japanese pumpkins (also called kabocha squash) are inexpensive, and they have a lovely hollow center already, so you just need to scoop out a light webbing of seeds. By the way, you can eat the pumpkin skin! In fact, I think it's one of the best bits!

COST PER SERVING: $0.63 | YIELD: 6-8 SERVINGS

FOR THE PUMPKIN

1 small gray or Japanese pumpkin (approximately 6½ lbs [2.8 kg])

2½ tbsp (40 ml) extra virgin olive oil

½ tsp salt

FOR THE FILLING

¼ cup (60 ml) extra virgin olive oil

1 red onion, diced

3 cloves garlic, roughly chopped

1 cup (200 g) uncooked long grain white rice, rinsed well and drained

½ cup (60 g) chopped walnuts

⅓ cup + 1 tbsp (60 g) golden raisins

2 tbsp (7 g) fresh parsley

1 tsp dried mint

1 tbsp (3 g) dried dill

2 cups (500 ml) water

1 tsp salt

Preheat the oven to 325°F (165°C).

To prepare the pumpkin, use a sharp knife to cut the top off the pumpkin. Use a spoon to hollow the inside out, removing all the seeds. Retain the top to use as a lid. Drizzle the olive oil inside the pumpkin, sprinkle the inside with salt, place the lid back on and bake for 30 minutes. The pumpkin should almost be tender the whole way through when pierced with a skewer. If it's completely tender, that is absolutely fine as well. It will depend on the size and shape of your pumpkin, but the next stage of cooking will ensure it is tender the whole way through if it's not quite there at this stage.

While the pumpkin is cooking, make the filling. Add the olive oil to a large saucepan and sauté the onion and garlic for 5 minutes. Add the rice and toast it for 3 to 4 minutes. Add the walnuts, raisins, parsley, mint, dill, water and salt and combine well. Cook on low with a lid on for 10 minutes. Remove from the heat and set aside until the pumpkin is ready. Fill the pumpkin with the rice mixture. Replace the lid and bake for 50 to 60 minutes, or until the rice is tender. Let the pumpkin rest for 10 minutes before slicing and serving.

CARAMELIZED ONION AND POTATO SPANISH TORTILLA

The first time I visited Spain was in 2011. I traveled with my good friend Nat, and I'll never forget ordering our first drink in Madrid at a small bar called El Tigre. The bartender handed us our sangria and we went to find a spot to stand before hearing him yell at us. We turned to find him holding plates piled high with food for us. We discovered that each drink you ordered came with a plate of food, to ensure you "lined your stomach" with something and didn't get too intoxicated. The plate featured the most incredibly delicious potato and onion Spanish tortilla atop a slice of bread that seemed like the least breakfast-y omelet I'd ever tasted. The onions were so sweet and caramelized, and the potato added such body and texture to the snack. Wholesome, unassuming, utterly delicious and the best 4 euros on dinner I'd ever spent.

COST PER SLICE: $0.25 | YIELD: 8 SNACK-SIZED SLICES

¼ cup (60 ml) extra virgin olive oil

1 large red onion, peeled and finely sliced

4 tsp (20 ml) balsamic vinegar

2 tbsp (25 g) brown sugar

3 potatoes (approximately 1 lb [500 g])

1 heaping tsp salt, divided

5 eggs

Cracked black pepper, to taste

Smoky Bell Pepper Sauce (page 118)

Heat a large nonstick skillet (you will need one with a lid) over medium-low heat and add the oil and onion. Cook for 10 minutes, or until softened. Add the balsamic vinegar and brown sugar and cook for 5 minutes, stirring occasionally. While this is cooking, slice the potatoes finely (think potato chips), leaving the skin on. Add them in with half the salt and place the lid on the pan. Cook for 20 minutes, stirring occasionally.

While the potatoes are cooking, beat the eggs in a bowl with the remaining salt and pepper.

After the potatoes have cooked, pour the eggs into the skillet, jiggling the skillet to even out the distribution of the eggs. Place the lid back on and cook until the eggs are firm and set. Take the pan off the heat and remove the lid. Let it rest for 4 to 5 minutes, then place a wooden board or large plate over the pan, and quickly and carefully flip the tortilla upside down onto it.

Slice and serve with my Smoky Bell Pepper Sauce (page 118).

ROASTED CARROTS WITH HONEY AND ZA'ATAR

Carrots are consistently one of the best bang-for-your-buck veggies you can buy. They're only around $1.00 for a 1-pound (454-g) bag, and there's minimal wastage. Roasted carrots are such a staple in Australian cooking, usually served with a Sunday roast, so I've taken some flavors from the Med to jazz up this classic. If you don't have za'atar, use ½ tablespoon (2 g) of dried thyme along with ½ tablespoon (5 g) of sesame seeds.

COST PER SERVING: $0.30 | YIELD: 4 SERVINGS

8 carrots (approximately 1½ lbs [700 g])

¼ cup (60 ml) extra virgin olive oil

2½ tbsp (40 ml) honey

1 heaping tbsp (3 g) za'atar

½ tsp salt

½ tsp cracked black pepper

Preheat the oven to 350°F (180°C).

Wash the carrots, and halve them if they are very large. Lay them in a baking dish and drizzle with the olive oil. Bake for 20 minutes. Remove them from the oven and drizzle them with the honey, then evenly sprinkle on the za'atar, salt and pepper. Return to the oven for 25 minutes, or until the carrots are wrinkly and tender.

FENNEL GRATINATI

Fennel is such an underrated vegetable. I think it's often pushed aside because many people don't know how it should be prepared. I have two favorite ways of serving fennel. One is to finely slice it and serve it raw with parsley and orange segments with an olive oil and vinegar dressing. The other is this way, baked in milk and nutmeg and topped with plenty of deliciously crispy, herby breadcrumbs. The milk tenderizes the fennel so it's gorgeous and soft and has just the most subtle delicious hint of aniseed throughout. All the ingredients are cheap and cheerful, especially when fennel is fresh and in season.

COST PER SERVING: $1.29 | YIELD: 4–6 SERVINGS

3 sprigs thyme

2 small fennel bulbs, trimmed and quartered

⅓ cup (80 ml) milk

½ tsp grated nutmeg

2 cups (220 g) breadcrumbs

Scant ⅔ cup (60 g) grated Parmesan

½ cup (60 g) finely chopped walnuts

1 tsp salt

½ tsp cracked black pepper

⅓ cup (80 ml) extra virgin olive oil

Preheat the oven to 325°F (165°C). Remove the leaves from the sprigs of thyme, and reserve. Discard the sprigs themselves.

Bring a pot of water to boil and add the fennel. Boil for 12 to 15 minutes, or until tender. Remove the fennel from the water with a slotted spoon and place the pieces in a single layer (a bit of overlapping is okay) in a large, oval baking dish.

While the fennel is boiling, combine the milk and nutmeg in a bowl and set aside. In another bowl, mix together the breadcrumbs, Parmesan, thyme leaves, walnuts, salt, pepper and olive oil. Pour the milk over the fennel, then spoon over the breadcrumb mixture. Bake for 35 to 40 minutes, or until the breadcrumbs are golden brown.

GARLICKY ARTICHOKE SALAD

Artichokes, like fennel, are one of those vegetables that really misses out. No one really knows too much about what to do with them. They're intimidating to prepare and only really affordable when they are in peak season because you don't really get too much out of them in terms of what is edible. So I use canned artichokes. They're already prepared, so you don't need to spend any time clipping away leaves or removing "hair" or "the choke" from the heart. They're already tender and still full of flavor; simply drain, rinse and slice. This salad recipe is one I've been making since my friend Yeliz brought it to a dinner we had at our friend Dil's house. Everyone raved about it, and it was the first time I'd had garlic and artichoke together, just by themselves. They are a total match made in heaven.

COST PER SERVING: $1.39 | YIELD: 4 SERVINGS, AS A SIDE

¼ cup (60 ml) extra virgin olive oil

2 (14-oz [400-g]) cans artichoke hearts, drained and rinsed

1 clove garlic, minced

3 tbsp (10 g) finely chopped fresh parsley

Juice of ½ lemon

Salt and cracked black pepper, to taste

Heat the olive oil in a skillet over low heat. Cut the artichokes in half, then add the artichoke pieces, minced garlic and parsley. Cook for 5 minutes, stirring occasionally. Transfer to a serving dish and serve with a squeeze of lemon and salt and pepper.

BAKED ZUCCHINI WITH PANGRATTATO

The biggest complaints I hear about vegetables are that they are tasteless and mushy. And if you boil the living daylights out of any vegetable, that is exactly what they will turn out like! It's rare to see a recipe from Greece or Italy that requires you to boil any vegetable. Seasoning, herbs, spices and texture are always added throughout the cooking process . . . and what a difference it makes to the whole eating experience! This zucchini recipe is such a gorgeous way to enjoy veggies baked to perfection and loaded up with salty, garlicky, crunchy, lip-smacking breadcrumbs that will have everyone licking their plates clean!

COST PER SERVING: $1.00 | YIELD: 4 SERVINGS

FOR THE ZUCCHINI

4 small green zucchinis, halved

Extra virgin olive oil, as needed

½ tsp salt

FOR THE PANGRATTATO

2 cups (220 g) breadcrumbs

¼ cup (25 g) grated Parmesan

2 cloves garlic, minced

4–5 sprigs thyme, leaves removed

⅓ cup (80 ml) extra virgin olive oil

Zest of 1 lemon

Preheat the oven to 350°F (180°C).

To make the zucchini, lay out the zucchinis flesh side up on a parchment-lined baking sheet. Drizzle with the olive oil and sprinkle with salt. Bake for 30 minutes, or until tender.

While the zucchinis are baking, make the pangrattato. Add the bread-crumbs, Parmesan, garlic, thyme, olive oil and lemon zest into a large skillet over medium heat. Toast, stirring every minute or so, for 5 to 6 minutes, or until the breadcrumbs are golden. Remove from the heat and carefully scoop the pangrattato into a bowl. If you leave it in the pan, it will continue to cook and might get a little burnt. Serve the zucchinis with a generous amount of pangrattato on top.

Luscious
LEGUMES, GLORIOUS
GRAINS AND PRIMO PASTA

A traditional Mediterranean diet focuses on a different kind of food pyramid where there are only four categories. Legumes and grains are in the same group as olive oil, fruits and vegetables, and this also happens to be the largest group. Eating legumes and grains regularly is beneficial for many different health outcomes as they are a great source of fiber, resistant starch, vitamins and minerals, and they generally have a low glycemic index. That means you will have sustained energy levels, and these foods will keep you feeling fuller for longer. These factors alone are amazing motivation to add them to your diet at every chance. In addition, eating legumes and grains regularly also helps keep the shopping budget down, as they are readily available, easy to prepare and incredibly economical, especially if you're cooking for a large family. You can find legumes and grains presoaked and canned—the ultimate "fast food"—or, for an even more affordable option, you can pick them up dried in bulk.

In this chapter, I show you how to transform your usual weekly rotation of recipes with luscious legumes and glorious grains. They are extremely versatile, which you will see as you begin cooking. You can use them in place of meat. You can use them to add texture and bite rather than utilizing cooking methods like frying. Or, you can enjoy them traditionally in pastas and risottos. I've used them in all these ways throughout the chapter to show you how to make recipes like Pumpkin and Sage Lasagna with Fresh Mozzarella (page 34), which is simply the best vegetarian lasagna ever that's made with golden roasted pumpkin, thick creamy layers of ricotta and sage-spiked olive oil béchamel; Herbed Pearl Couscous with Dried Figs and Pomegranate (page 46), which is decadent and bejeweled; and a cheap and cheerful Chickpea Freekeh Salad with Lemon, Celery and Parsley (page 50) that is out of this world.

PUMPKIN AND SAGE LASAGNA WITH FRESH MOZZARELLA

Everyone needs a good lasagna recipe in their life, and this is my new number one. It's super affordable and very easy to make. This recipe freezes so well, so you can double the recipe, make two at once and freeze one for a quick and easy dinner for later on.

COST PER SERVING: $1.43 | YIELD: 6 SERVINGS

FOR THE PUMPKIN

Approximately 2 lbs (1 kg) pumpkin, peeled and cut into ¼-inch (6-mm)-thick slices

Extra virgin olive oil, for drizzling

Salt and cracked black pepper, as needed

FOR THE BÉCHAMEL SAUCE (WHITE SAUCE)

¼ cup (60 ml) extra virgin olive oil

25–30 large sage leaves, chopped

⅓ cup (45 g) all-purpose flour

2 cups (500 ml) milk

¼ tsp salt

¼ tsp cracked black pepper

¼ tsp nutmeg

¼ cup (25 g) grated Parmesan

FOR THE LASAGNA

⅔ cup (100 g) feta cheese

1½ cups (350 g) ricotta cheese

¾ cup (185 ml) water

1 (9-oz [250-g]) package of lasagna noodles (sheets) (you won't need them all)

1 (7-oz [198-g]) mozzarella ball, torn

Preheat the oven to 350°F (180°C). To make the pumpkin, place the pumpkin slices on a parchment-lined baking sheet. Drizzle with a little olive oil and sprinkle with salt and pepper. Bake for 20 minutes, or until the slices are soft. When you take the pumpkin from the oven, remember to leave the oven on so you can bake your lasagna.

While the pumpkin is baking, prepare the béchamel sauce. Heat the olive oil in a small saucepan over medium-low heat. Add the sage leaves. Fry for 3 to 4 minutes, then remove the sage from the oil with a slotted spoon. Set it aside. Add the flour to the hot oil and combine it with a whisk. Add the milk, a little bit at a time, whisking until you have a uniform consistency and the mixture begins to thicken each time. Then add more milk and whisk again until all the milk is used. Add the salt, pepper, nutmeg, fried sage leaves and Parmesan and whisk until the béchamel is like thin pancake batter. Set aside.

To assemble the lasagna, mix together the feta, ricotta and water in a bowl and set aside. I use a 17 x 25 x 5–centimeter lasagna baking dish for my lasagna, and I always have three layers of pasta. The closest US size dish is 7 x 10½ inches (18 x 27 cm). Spoon a little sauce into the bottom of the lasagna dish, then layer the noodles, being careful not to overlap them, followed by an even layer of pumpkin. Add one-third of the ricotta mixture. It might be thick, so spread it out as best you can, but it doesn't need to be perfect because it will melt and spread as it bakes. Finally, pour one-third of the sauce, and then repeat until you have three layers of everything. The top layer will be sauce, but you can always add an additional layer of lasagna noodles on top if you have them. Add the mozzarella cheese on top of the lasagna. Bake for 25 to 30 minutes, or until the cheese on top is golden. Once the lasagna is cooked, let it sit for 5 minutes before slicing and serving. You can add additional seasoning once served if you'd like.

RICOTTA GNOCCHI

This recipe is a weekly staple in our house. It's so light and delicate and incredibly easy to make. There's no special equipment required or any pricey ingredients, and it barely requires any preparation—unlike potato gnocchi—to get that pillowy soft texture. I teach this recipe in my cooking classes, and everyone is always surprised at its simplicity and just how good it tastes once cooked. You can serve these boiled with my Rustic Walnut Pesto (page 121), which is my absolute favorite way to have them, or you can boil them, then finish them off in a pan with some olive oil to crisp up the outsides.

COST PER SERVING: $1.11 | YIELD: 4 SERVINGS

2½ cups (600 g) ricotta cheese

¾ cup + 1 tbsp (80 g) grated Parmesan

1 tsp cracked black pepper

2 eggs

2 cups (240 g) all-purpose flour, plus extra as needed

Begin by bringing a large pot of salted water to boil. While the water is heating up, begin making your gnocchi.

Place the ricotta, Parmesan, pepper and eggs in a large bowl and combine very well with a metal spoon. It should be quite smooth and creamy, so this may require a little elbow grease. Add the flour and work it into the ricotta mixture using the back of a spoon until just combined. Be careful not to overmix or else the gnocchi will end up a little rubbery.

Once the dough has come together, divide it into four pieces. Sprinkle some extra flour onto a clean surface and roll each piece of dough out with your hands into a long sausage about ½ to ¾ inch (1.2 to 1.9 cm) thick. Then cut the "sausages" into ½-inch (1.2-cm)-thick pieces with a butter knife. If the dough is sticky, dip your knife into some flour and it will help. Repeat with the remaining dough.

Cook the gnocchi in the boiling, salted water until they rise to the top. Once they have risen, cook for another 30 seconds, then strain and serve with any of the sauces in the Good-for-You (and Your Wallet) Sauces, Spreads and Dips chapter (page 113).

GORGEOUS GREEN PAN PIZZA

This could not be a cookbook about Mediterranean-style cooking if it didn't have a pizza in it! This version is one of my all-time favorite Friday night dinners and much healthier for you than takeout, with homemade dough, a little fresh mozzarella, veggie-packed pesto and more veggies on top. I love cooking this in a casserole pan because it makes for the best deep-dish style pizza, but feel free to just cook it like a normal pizza on a baking sheet or divide the dough up into little bases for a healthy snack or lunch.

COST PER SERVING: $2.18 | YIELD: 4 SERVINGS

Just under 1 cup (220 ml) warm water

2 tsp (8 g) dry quick-rising yeast

1 tbsp (14 g) brown sugar

1 tsp salt

3¼ cups (400 g) all-purpose flour

2½ tbsp (40 ml) extra virgin olive oil, plus extra as needed

¾ cup (180 ml) Three Greens Pesto (page 122)

1 (7-oz [198-g]) mozzarella ball, torn

1 bunch of broccolini, trimmed

½ red onion, peeled and finely sliced

Lemon zest, for serving

Add the warm water, yeast and brown sugar into a bowl of a stand mixer fitted with a dough hook. Combine for 30 seconds, or until the mixture looks opaque. Add the salt, flour and olive oil and knead for 4 to 5 minutes on medium speed, or until the dough is combined, smooth and elastic. Place the dough into an oiled bowl and cover with plastic wrap or a plate for at least 1 hour so it can double in size.

When you're ready to cook, preheat the oven to 400°F (200°C), and drizzle some olive oil into a wide-based, oven-safe pan. Remove the cover off the dough and punch your fist into the middle of the dough to collapse it. Then take it out of the bowl and place it into the pan pressing it out into a round shape to fill the whole bottom of the pan. Spread the pesto over the dough as your base, then add pieces of mozzarella followed by the broccolini and red onion. Place the pizza into the oven and cook for 20 to 25 minutes, or until the cheese is golden. You might like to leave it a little longer to really crisp it up. Serve with a fresh zesting of lemon over the top.

SPAGHETTI WITH CAPERS, CHERRY TOMATOES AND LEMON

Spaghetti is one of those foods I'll never tire of. I've eaten it multiple times a week my entire life. My husband, Isaac, jokes I probably have spaghetti running through my veins! This is one of the fastest dishes to make, as you basically throw it together with a few things from the fridge. I refer to this at home as my lazy dinner because it takes zero effort and minimal time. If I have some tuna in the pantry, I like to add that in too just before serving for something a little extra. If you're out of cherry tomatoes, you can substitute regular ones or even canned tomatoes.

COST PER SERVING: $1.10 | YIELD: 4 SERVINGS

¼ cup (60 ml) extra virgin olive oil

¼ cup (40 g) capers

12 oz (340 g) uncooked spaghetti

2⅔ cups (400 g) halved cherry tomatoes

Juice of 1–2 lemons, to taste

Salt, to taste

Crushed red pepper flakes, to taste (optional)

Heat a large pot of salted water over high heat. When the water has almost reached boiling point, place a skillet over medium heat, and add the olive oil and capers.

Once the water is boiling, add the spaghetti and cook until it's al dente, per package instructions.

While the pasta is cooking, sauté the capers for 2 to 3 minutes, or until the capers start to pop. Add the tomatoes, and cook for 3 to 4 minutes. Transfer the cooked spaghetti to the skillet. Squeeze the lemon juice over the pasta, season with salt and red pepper flakes if you like a little heat and use tongs to mix the sauce through the spaghetti before serving.

PESTO RISOTTO

I firmly believe that it's essential to have a good, basic risotto recipe. By cooking a delicious and reliable base recipe, you can add anything you might have on hand. Think roasted pumpkin chunks, sautéed mushrooms with a little thyme, a liberal splash of Bolognese mixed through before serving or a cup of pesto from the fridge. You can add any pesto (or sauce for that matter!) from the Good-for-You (and Your Wallet) Sauces, Spreads and Dips chapter (page 113) into this recipe to have yourself a comforting, wholesome bowl of risotto for pennies on the dollar.

COST PER SERVING: $0.80 | YIELD: 4 SERVINGS

6¼ cups (1.5 L) chicken or vegetable stock

¼ cup (60 ml) extra virgin olive oil

1 yellow (brown) onion, peeled and diced

4 cloves garlic, roughly chopped

2 cups (400 g) uncooked arborio rice

⅓ cup (80 ml) dry white wine (optional)

1 cup (240 ml) Three Greens Pesto (page 122)

Parmesan cheese, for serving

Place the stock in a saucepan over low heat.

While the stock is heating, heat the oil in a large saucepan over a medium heat and cook the onion for 5 minutes, or until it has softened. Add the garlic and cook for 2 minutes. Add the rice and toast it for 2 to 3 minutes before adding the wine (if using). If you added the wine, stir continuously for 2 minutes, or until the wine has absorbed into the rice and it has thickened. Add a ladle of stock to the rice, stirring constantly until the stock has been absorbed, 3 to 4 minutes. Continue adding stock and stirring the rice until all of the stock has been used.

With the last ladle of stock, add the pesto and continue stirring until the risotto has thickened again and the rice is tender. You can add a little more stock if the rice isn't al dente by the time you've used it all. Serve in bowls with a generous grating of Parmesan cheese.

ROASTED GRAPE BRUSCHETTA

Grapes never really tickled my fancy when I was growing up. There was always a better fruit to choose. That was until I went to Italy just after finishing high school and found myself ordering a grape focaccia from a tiny little focacceria. It cost 1.50 euros and came out in a paper bag, piping hot with the grapes still sizzling and oozing on top of the salty dough. I only needed one bite to realize how incredible that little fruit I never cared much for could be. This bruschetta recipe showcases grapes in all their delicious, thrifty glory and transports me straight back to the day I had my first grape focaccia with loads of sweet, sticky black grapes, a generous helping of creamy ricotta and the satisfying crunch of olive oil–soaked bread.

COST PER SERVING: $0.70 | YIELD: 8 SERVINGS, AS A STARTER

1 large bunch black or red seedless grapes (approximately 1 lb [500 g])

¼ cup (60 ml) extra virgin olive oil, divided

2 sprigs rosemary

Salt, as needed

8 slices crusty bread (Vienna, pane di casa or your preferred loaf)

Approximately 1⅔ cups (400 g) ricotta cheese

Cracked black pepper, to taste

Preheat the oven to 350°F (180°C).

Pick the grapes off their stems and place them onto a parchment-lined baking sheet. Drizzle with 1 tablespoon (15 ml) of olive oil, tear the leaves off the rosemary stems and add them to the grapes, and season with a pinch of salt. Roast the grapes for 25 minutes, and set them aside to cool slightly. You can even let them go completely cold. The flavor will be amazing either way.

Generously brush the slices of bread on both sides with the remaining olive oil, then place them on a griddle pan over medium heat. Cook each side for 2 to 3 minutes, or until golden and beginning to char. Spread each slice with a large spoonful of ricotta and top with the roasted grapes. Season with salt and pepper to taste, and serve the bruschetta while the bread is still hot and crispy.

HERBED PEARL COUSCOUS WITH DRIED FIGS AND POMEGRANATE

Figs and pomegranates were featured heavily in ancient Greek cuisine, usually eaten as dessert alongside other fruits. Figs were also often dried and eaten as an appetizer with wine before dinner, which sounds like an utterly simple and delicious starter to me. These days, Greek recipes still utilize figs and pomegranates, but not just for dessert or with wine. They are used in plenty of sweets and salads and are even added to savory dishes. They add a burst of brightness in both color and flavor and make this grain salad extra special.

COST PER SERVING: $2.15 | YIELD: 4 SERVINGS

2 cups (320 g) uncooked pearl couscous

4⅔ cups (1.125 L) chicken or vegetable stock

¼ cup (60 ml) extra virgin olive oil

Juice of 1 lemon

⅔ cup (80 g) roughly chopped walnuts

5 dried figs (140 g), cut into chunks

2 tbsp (11 g) chopped mint leaves

3 tbsp (10 g) chopped parsley

Jewels of 1 pomegranate

Salt and cracked black pepper, to taste

Combine the couscous and stock in a large saucepan over medium-low heat. Place the lid on the pan and cook for 10 to 12 minutes, or until the stock is absorbed and the couscous is tender. You can add a little water if it's not quite tender once the stock is absorbed.

Fluff up the couscous with a spoon, drizzle the olive oil over it and stir. Add the lemon juice, walnuts, figs, mint, parsley, pomegranate jewels, salt and pepper to the pan and combine very well, seasoning to taste. Serve in a large bowl or platter with Bulgur and Lamb Kofta (page 104) or BBQ Lemon and Herb Chicken (page 95).

WARM FARRO SALAD

Farro is a type of wheat grain typically found throughout Italy but is also available around the world now that its popularity has grown. It has a beautiful texture, remaining slightly chewy when cooked and adding body and density to any salad or soup. It also has a beautiful nutty flavor that I think pairs just spectacularly with carrots, herbs and almonds. While farro is more expensive than other cereals and grains, a little goes a long way, making it an affordable addition to the pantry.

COST PER SERVING: $1.49 | YIELD: 4 SERVINGS

2¼ cups (300 g) farro

3⅛ cups (750 ml) water

3 carrots

¼ cup (60 ml) extra virgin olive oil

½ tsp salt, plus extra as needed

⅓ cup (21 g) chopped parsley

2 tbsp (6 g) dried dill

1 tsp sumac, plus extra for garnish

⅓ cup (45 g) roasted almonds

¼ tsp cracked black pepper

1 cup (285 g) Greek yogurt

Juice of ½–1 lemon, to taste

Preheat the oven to 350°F (180°C).

Place the farro into a saucepan with the water, put the lid on and simmer over medium-low heat until all the water is absorbed and the farro is tender. While the farro is cooking, trim the ends of the carrots, and cut them in half (across the carrot). Cut each half into quarters, lengthways. Arrange these in a single layer on a parchment-lined baking sheet. Drizzle with the oil and sprinkle with salt. Bake for 20 to 25 minutes, or until softened. While the carrots are cooking, add the cooked farro to a large bowl to cool slightly and add the parsley, dill, sumac, almonds, ½ teaspoon of salt and pepper and combine.

To make the dressing, mix together the yogurt, lemon juice and a sprinkling of salt in a small bowl. Spoon the farro salad onto a serving plate, top with cooked carrots and any cooking juices, then dollop the dressing and sprinkle sumac on top to serve.

CHICKPEA FREEKEH SALAD WITH LEMON, CELERY AND PARSLEY

Freekeh is another species of wheat that has been around for centuries and is featured in traditional Levant, Anatolian, Lebanese, Egyptian and Middle Eastern cuisine as well as many others. It's not conventionally Mediterranean, but I began using it when I was learning how to cook Turkish food and fell for its unique flavor. The freekeh grain is roasted and rubbed to give it its distinct earthy, nutty taste and its firm, chewy outer layer. And I really love it together with the celery, golden raisins and chickpeas in this salad. The flavor is magnificent, and each bite is filled with something new and interesting, making it a salad to bookmark.

COST PER SERVING: $1.13 | YIELD: 4 SERVINGS

1 cup (225 g) freekeh

2⅔ cups (660 ml) water

3 celery ribs, leaves removed

½ small red onion, peeled and diced

Just under 1 cup (130 g) golden raisins

1 (14.5-oz [411-g]) can chickpeas, drained and rinsed

¼ cup (16 g) fresh parsley

Juice of 1 lemon

¼ cup (60 ml) extra virgin olive oil

Salt and cracked black pepper, to taste

Place the freekeh into a saucepan with the water, put the lid on and simmer over medium-low heat until all the water is absorbed and the freekeh is tender.

While the freekeh is cooking, finely slice the celery and add it to a large bowl. Add the onion, raisins, chickpeas and parsley and combine well.

Once the freekeh is cooked, cool slightly and add it to the bowl. Dress with the lemon juice, olive oil, salt and pepper, and adjust the seasoning to taste. Serve warm.

SHEPHERD'S SALAD WITH WHITE BEANS

I first had this salad while writing my thesis on Turkish culinary culture, and I soon found out that this salad was seemingly the equivalent to the Australian lettuce, tomato and cucumber salads I grew up eating . . . except with a lot more flavor and goodness. The addition of cannellini beans adds protein, which will keep you feeling fuller for longer while still enjoying a completely plant-based dish. I love having this with my Bulgur and Lamb Kofta (page 104) because it always elicits the feeling that summer isn't too far away.

COST PER SERVING: $1.56 | YIELD: 4 SERVINGS

1 large red bell pepper (capsicum)

1 Lebanese cucumber

1⅔ cups (250 g) cherry tomatoes

1 (14-oz [400-g]) can cannellini beans

⅔ cup (100 g) feta

1 small red onion, finely diced

¼ cup (16 g) chopped parsley

3–4 sprigs dill

Juice of 1 lemon

¼ cup (60 ml) extra virgin olive oil

Salt and cracked black pepper, to taste

Remove the core from the bell pepper and finely dice up the rest. Cut the cucumber into thick rounds, then cut the rounds into quarters. Halve the cherry tomatoes. Add the pepper, cucumber and tomatoes to a large bowl.

Drain and rinse the beans in a colander, shake any excess water off and add to the bowl. Crumble the feta into the bowl and add the onion, parsley and dill. Dress with the lemon juice, olive oil, salt and pepper, then mix well to serve.

ROASTED EGGPLANT SALAD WITH BRAISED CHICKPEAS AND CITRUS YOGURT

This recipe is so satisfying, with tender roasted eggplant in each mouthful, that delicious sweetness of sautéed garlic, a squeeze of fresh lemon and tart Greek yogurt to cut through it. I have bulked the dish up with a luscious, glistening topping of softened onions and chickpeas, but you could use rice or any other legume if you have it already on hand. By doing this, and using just a few eggplants and not much else, this dish is fabulously frugal and filling.

COST PER SERVING: $1.95 | YIELD: 4-6 SERVINGS

FOR THE EGGPLANT

¼ cup (60 ml) extra virgin olive oil, plus extra for drizzling

1 yellow (brown) onion, finely sliced

1 (14-oz [400-g]) can chickpeas, drained and rinsed

½ cup (125 ml) water

1 tsp salt

6 Lebanese eggplants (petite version of regular eggplant)

FOR THE YOGURT SAUCE

1½ cups (430 g) Greek yogurt

½ tsp salt

Juice of 1 lemon

Sumac (optional)

Crushed red pepper flakes (optional)

Fresh mint, to taste (optional)

Preheat the oven to 350°F (180°C).

To make the eggplant, heat a large saucepan over medium heat and add the olive oil. Add the onion and sauté for 5 minutes, or until it is softened. Add the chickpeas, water and salt. Stir to combine. Place the lid on the pan and cook for 15 minutes. Remove the lid and cook for 10 minutes, or until the mixture has only a small amount of moisture left. Remove the pan from the heat. While the onions and chickpeas are cooking, cut the eggplants in half lengthways. Lay them flesh side up on a parchment-lined baking sheet and drizzle with olive oil. Bake for 15 to 20 minutes, or until soft.

To make the yogurt sauce, combine the yogurt, salt, lemon juice, sumac (if using) and red pepper flakes (if using) in a bowl and mix well. To serve, place the eggplant on a long platter in a single layer, spoon the chickpeas over the eggplant and place a dollop of yogurt sauce on top. You can add some fresh mint leaves or extra sumac if you like (which I highly recommend!).

ORZO SALAD WITH CUCUMBER, TOMATO AND BASIL

Pasta salads were such a big deal at barbecues when I was growing up, but I'm not actually sure I've ever really seen a pasta salad anywhere in Italy! It's probably quite obvious that this isn't a traditional recipe, but that doesn't make it any less tasty! I took a few staple ingredients of Mediterranean food and combined them with al dente orzo to create this quick and easy side dish that I just love. And I know your next barbecue guests will too.

COST PER SERVING: $1.55 | YIELD: 4–6 SERVINGS

1⅓ cups (135 g) orzo (risoni pasta)

2 Lebanese cucumbers

1⅔ cups (250 g) cherry tomatoes

½ cup (15 g) basil leaves

½ cup (95 g) pitted kalamata olives

¼ cup (60 ml) extra virgin olive oil

Juice of 1 lemon

Salt and cracked black pepper, to taste

Feta or goat cheese, for serving (optional)

Cook the orzo in boiling salted water until it's al dente. Strain and rinse with cold water in a colander. Place the cooked orzo into a large mixing bowl.

Slice the cucumbers into thick rounds and cut each round into quarters. Add these to the bowl. Halve the cherry tomatoes and add to the bowl. Roughly tear up the basil leaves and toss into the bowl. Add the olives. Drizzle the olive oil over the ingredients and add the lemon juice as well.

Season with a little salt and pepper and serve. You might also like to add some feta or goat cheese to this salad to make it extra special.

BRAISED WHITE BEANS WITH ONION AND PARSLEY

White beans are a feature throughout Mediterranean cooking, especially in Greek and Italian cuisine. They are very economical, easy to prepare—especially if you buy them already soaked in a can—and incredibly good for you. This recipe is like a winter salad, because salads aren't just for warm weather. It's so cozy and nourishing, and I like to serve it the Italian way with sausages added in with the stock so they cook through and can be served as a one-pot dinner.

COST PER SERVING: $0.37 | YIELD: 4 SERVINGS

⅓ cup (80 ml) extra virgin olive oil

1 yellow (brown) onion, peeled and finely sliced

3 cloves garlic, roughly chopped

2½ tbsp (10 g) chopped parsley

2 (14-oz [400-g]) cans cannellini beans, drained and rinsed

½ cup (125 ml) chicken or vegetable stock

Cracked black pepper, to taste

Heat a shallow saucepan over low heat and add the olive oil, onion and garlic. Cook for 15 minutes with a lid on until they are softened and sweated down.

Add the parsley, beans and stock and cook over low heat for 25 to 30 minutes, stirring occasionally and making sure it doesn't stick. If it begins to stick, add a little water. Serve hot with freshly cracked black pepper.

Super SIMPLE AND SATISFYING SOUPS

When I see soup on a restaurant menu, I automatically skip it. I know I shouldn't, but I always find that I'm disappointed. Nothing quite lives up to the soups my mum and nonna would have bubbling away on the stove when I was growing up. The incredible layers of flavor were built with the most basic ingredients and pantry staples, like legumes and vegetables (that also happen to be mainstays of the Mediterranean cuisine), and seasoned with just salt, pepper, herbs from the garden and some Parmesan. These simple ingredients can create an endless combination of healthy, wholesome soups that are incredibly nourishing and taste phenomenal.

My sister and I used to beg my mum to make us *riso e patate*, which is half risotto, half soup and incredibly nourishing. It's quite a flexible recipe, and as long as you have celery and a potato, the flavor will always be there. My nonna, having grown up in Veneto where this *cucina povera* recipe comes from, made her version years ago using just what she had in the fridge. And as with all of her recipes, she didn't write it down but just continued to make it from memory, tasting as she went. By the time my mum started making it, she had written down bits and pieces that were important to remember, but still no recipe. So, when it came time to writing this chapter and re-creating Riso e Patate (page 66) and the other recipes properly, I took my time measuring, comparing, tasting and revising until it was perfect so you could cook it without a hitch and enjoy the warm delicious coziness I adore.

For this chapter, I wanted to share some of my family recipes, which have been passed down from my nonna to my mum and now to me, as well as some recipes I learned while studying Turkish culinary culture and visiting friends in Istanbul. These soups taste like home to me and are so simple and inexpensive that I hope they will take up a loving place in your kitchen as well.

PASTA E FAGIOLI

In 2019, I visited Bologna with my good friend Camilla. It was November, so it was dreary and it rained the whole time. But it really didn't bother us because we found so much comfort in bowl after bowl of *pasta e fagioli* (pasta and beans). We wandered into this jam-packed, hole-in-the-wall restaurant filled with students and locals alike and squeezed ourselves into a tiny table while furiously taking off our wet, soggy layers of clothing. We quickly ordered lunch and wine (of course) and proceeded to "ooh" and "aah" over every bite of our veggie- and olive oil–laden bowls. We walked out of there with full bellies and flushed cheeks, having only parted with a few euros each. The best kind of lunch, if you ask me.

COST PER SERVING: $1.15 | YIELD: 4 SERVINGS

⅓ cup (80 ml) extra virgin olive oil, plus extra for serving

1 large yellow (brown) onion, peeled and finely diced

4 celery ribs, including the leaves, finely diced

3 large potatoes, peeled and diced

6¼ cups (1.5 L) chicken or vegetable stock

1 cup (250 ml) passata (tomato puree)

2 (14-oz [400-g]) cans borlotti beans

2 Parmesan rinds (optional)

7 oz (198 g) pasta of your choice, from orzo to fettucine to shells

Salt and cracked black pepper, to taste

Freshly grated Parmesan, for serving

Heat the olive oil in a large heavy saucepan and sauté the onion, celery and potatoes over medium heat until the onion is translucent and softened. Add the stock, passata, beans and Parmesan rinds (if using), and simmer for 15 minutes.

Add the pasta and cook until al dente, stirring occasionally. Remove the Parmesan rinds and season the soup with salt and pepper, to taste. Serve with freshly grated Parmesan and a generous drizzle of extra virgin olive oil.

ACQUACOTTA (VEGETABLE AND OLIVE OIL SOUP)

Acquacotta in Italian means "cooked water." That's because this soup was originally known as a peasant food that was made by cooking any odds and ends available in water seasoned only with a splash of tomato. Traditionally, it was cooked with bread in the soup as well, so any leftover stale bread that was too hard to chew could still be eaten. It's incredibly affordable to make and you can really add anything you might have in the fridge to it. So don't think this is a hard and fast recipe. Feel free to add a little bacon or pancetta, some mushrooms or even some canned beans. And if poaching eggs isn't your strength—it wasn't mine for years until my good friend Ebony recently showed me the trick—just add a boiled egg instead.

COST PER SERVING: $0.88 | YIELD: 4 SERVINGS

¼ cup (60 ml) extra virgin olive oil

1 yellow (brown) onion, peeled and diced

3 cloves garlic, roughly chopped

1 celery rib, including the leaves, sliced

1 large carrot, skin on and diced

2 chard leaves, stalk trimmed and roughly sliced

⅓ cup (66 g) crushed tomatoes

8⅓ cups (2 L) chicken or vegetable stock

4 eggs

¼ cup (60 ml) white vinegar

Slices of toasted or stale bread, torn into pieces

Salt and cracked black pepper, to taste

Parmesan cheese, to taste (optional)

Heat the olive oil in a heavy saucepan over medium heat. Add the onion, garlic, celery and carrot. Sauté for about 10 minutes. Add the chard and sauté for 2 to 3 minutes, or until it has wilted. Add the tomatoes and stock, and simmer for 20 minutes.

While the soup is cooking, crack the eggs individually into small cups. Heat a small saucepan of water and add the vinegar. Once the water has boiled, turn the heat down so it continues to simmer but doesn't have a rolling boil with lots of bubbles. Use a metal spoon to carefully and quickly stir the water so a little whirlpool begins to form. Drop one of the eggs into the middle of the whirlpool and poach it for 4 to 5 minutes. Remove the poached egg with a slotted spoon and set aside on a plate. Repeat this process with the remaining eggs.

Serve the soup in a large bowl topped with a poached egg and torn bread. Season with salt and pepper to taste. I also really love sprinkling some Parmesan cheese on top.

RISO E PATATE

This is the kind of soup that speaks to my heart. It's robust and filling and does not skimp on flavor in the slightest. It's so nourishing, and in my opinion, it's particularly nourishing for your soul and your wallet—costing just pennies to make. Created by my nonna, this is the first time the recipe has been written down and shared, and I couldn't be happier in doing so!

COST PER SERVING: $0.73 | YIELD: 4 SERVINGS

3–4 celery ribs, including the leaves, roughly chopped

2 large potatoes, peeled and diced

1 large yellow (brown) onion, diced

½ cup (100 g) crushed tomatoes

4 cups (1 L) water

4⅛ cups (1 L) chicken stock

1¾ cups (345 g) uncooked arborio rice

Salt and cracked black pepper, to taste

Freshly grated Parmesan, for serving

Place the celery, potatoes, onion, tomatoes and water in a large saucepan and bring it to a boil with the lid on. Continue to slowly boil it until the veggies are softened, about 20 minutes. Remove the saucepan from the heat. While the soup is cooking, heat the stock up in another saucepan.

Blend the soup with a handheld immersion blender until smooth. Add the rice along with a ladleful of stock. Stir regularly until the soup begins to thicken, then pour in the rest of the stock and continue to simmer on low heat until the rice is tender, approximately 20 minutes. Season with salt and pepper if needed, and serve piping hot with lots of grated Parmesan and more black pepper.

RED LENTIL SOUP

Dried red lentils are one of the most cost-effective ingredients in my pantry. A large bag is just a couple of dollars. They're an incredible lentil to use not only in this soup but also in salads and stews because they are the quickest cooking lentil. They don't need to be soaked before cooking, and 15 minutes is all it takes for them to cook through and absorb all the delicious herbs and spices you might be pairing them with.

COST PER SERVING: $0.31 | YIELD: 4 SERVINGS

⅓ cup (80 ml) extra virgin olive oil

1 red onion, peeled and diced

1 large carrot, skin on and diced

2 tbsp (32 g) tomato paste

1 tbsp (16 g) harissa

1 whole tomato, diced

¾ cup (155 g) red lentils

6¼ cups (1.5 L) vegetable stock

½ tsp salt, plus extra as needed

¼ tsp cracked black pepper, plus extra as needed

Greek yogurt, for serving (optional)

Heat the olive oil in a large saucepan, and sauté the onion and carrot over medium heat for 10 minutes, or until the onion is translucent and the carrot is tender.

Add the tomato paste, harissa and tomato and fry off for 2 minutes or so before adding the lentils, stock, salt and pepper. Stir to loosen the lentils, then cover and simmer for 30 minutes. Season with salt and pepper to taste, and serve alone or with a dollop of Greek yogurt.

FIRE-ROASTED BELL PEPPER SOUP

My love of chargrilled bell peppers (capsicums) continues with this recipe, and fittingly so with a Mediterranean diet always highlighting the most delicious ways to enjoy its most abundant food group: vegetables. This soup is perfect for warming you up top to toes during winter with an impressive combination of sweet flame-grilled bell peppers, fiery harissa and a handful of kitchen staples to keep the budget in check. If you prefer a milder dish, simply omit the harissa.

COST PER SERVING: $1.45 | YIELD: 4 SERVINGS

4 large red bell peppers (capsicums)

¼ cup (60 ml) extra virgin olive oil

1 red onion, peeled and diced

4 cloves garlic, roughly chopped

½–1 tsp harissa

1 (14-oz [400-g]) can crushed tomatoes

6¼ cups (1.5 L) chicken or vegetable stock

Crusty bread, for serving

Three Greens Pesto (page 122), for serving

Salt, to taste

Turn the gas of one of your burners to medium heat, and carefully place a bell pepper directly over the flame using metal tongs. If you don't have a gas grill, you can use a cooking torch. The flame will begin to blister and burn the bell pepper skin, and this is exactly what we want. Once the skin has blackened, carefully turn the pepper, repeating until the entire pepper has black skin. Place the charred pepper into a large bowl and cover it with a plate to sweat. Char the remaining peppers, then pop them into the bowl to sweat as well for 20 or so minutes. Peel the charred peppers over the sink. Place the blackened skins into the bowl and the soft, tender grilled peppers onto a clean plate. Pull the stalk and seeds out while you're peeling them. If the charred skin is sticking a little bit, turn the tap on and rinse the pepper while peeling.

Heat the olive oil in a heavy saucepan, and sauté the onion and garlic for 5 minutes, until the onion begins to turn translucent. Add the harissa and fry off for a minute. Add in the bell peppers (no need to cut them up), tomatoes and stock. Simmer for 30 minutes, then blend the soup smooth with a handheld immersion blender or in a blender. Serve with crusty bread, a spoonful of Three Greens Pesto (page 122) and some salt, if needed.

Seafood FOR ALL SEASONS
(NOT JUST SUMMER!)

The most prominent animal protein in the Mediterranean diet is seafood. It's a great source of protein but is also a wonderful source of healthy fats such as omega-3 fatty acids, which are an important component in the body's cell membranes. Seafood is also generally quite low in saturated fat, unlike a lot of other animal proteins, making it a healthy choice you can enjoy more regularly.

I have never eaten better seafood than what I have had on my trips to the Mediterranean. I have such strong memories of the fresh oysters off the back of a boat in Spain, the spaghetti alle vongole in Italy and the amazing salted cod in Portugal and Croatia. Just thinking about them takes me straight back and makes my mouth water. The first time I had octopus cooked over charcoal in Portugal was life changing. The great thing about seafood is that it is so versatile and varied, and thanks to my recipes in this chapter, you don't need a trip to the Mediterranean to enjoy everything they have to offer! From prawns to oysters, fish to octopus . . . the possibilities are endless.

There is a misconception that seafood is unaffordable. When you go to a restaurant and browse the menu, seafood is almost always the most expensive item. But it doesn't have to be. I'm here to show you that enjoying seafood can be done on the regular and within budget. Imagine adding creamy, decadent Garlic Prawn Risotto (page 77) laced with lemon zest to your weekly meal planning, fresh Grilled Sardines with Parsley, Lemon Zest and Tomato Seeds on Charred Bread (page 78) or even an incredibly scrumptious dish of Lemon and Caper Fish Piccata (page 82) the next time you have friends around for dinner.

None of the recipes in this chapter are difficult to manage, hopefully alleviating any anxiety you might have if you're a first-time seafood cook. And I've chosen seafood that doesn't require much groundwork at all, so you can simply add it to the dish without the daunting task of cleaning and preparing it. Seafood has never been easier or more accessible!

SPAGHETTI ALLE VONGOLE

Last year, we spent a while on the Amalfi coast, where I am absolutely certain I ate my weight in spaghetti alle vongole, which only got better with every single bite. You might know *vongole* as clams or *pippies*, as we call them in Australia, or you might've seen this very popular dish on a restaurant menu somewhere. It is popular, and with very good reason, as it's an ingenuous use of basic ingredients—olive oil, garlic, tomato—to complement the subtle salty sweetness of freshly cooked vongole. You can pick up clams at the market very reasonably, making this stunning seafood recipe one you can whip up a little more often.

COST PER SERVING: $2.96 | YIELD: 4 SERVINGS

⅓ cup (80 ml) extra virgin olive oil

8 cloves garlic, minced and finely chopped

2 tomatoes, diced

12 oz (340 g) uncooked spaghetti

⅓ cup (80 ml) dry white wine

21 oz (590 g) clams (vongole)

⅓ cup (20 g) parsley

Salt and cracked black pepper, to taste

Bring a large pot of salted water to a boil so you can cook the spaghetti. Once the water is almost boiling, add the olive oil to a large skillet over medium heat and sauté the garlic for 1 minute. Add the tomatoes and let them simmer for about 2 minutes. You can cook the spaghetti to al dente while the tomatoes are cooking.

Add the wine and clams to the tomatoes and watch the clams cook and open up. Once the spaghetti is cooked (about 8 minutes), carefully drain it in a colander and add it to the skillet along with the parsley, stirring to coat the spaghetti in sauce. Season with salt and pepper and serve.

NOTE: If some clams do not open after 10 or so minutes of cooking, throw them away. You only want to eat the ones that have opened up by themselves. This dish is traditionally served with the clams in the shell. You can of course take them all out of the shell if you prefer.

GARLIC PRAWN RISOTTO

There was never a better duo than garlic and prawns, and they absolutely sing together in this risotto. Prawns are normally seen as a luxury ingredient, but we are only adding a small amount into this recipe because we want the flavor without the steep grocery bill. If you have a larger budget to play with, feel free to add in more, but you will not be missing out should you follow the recipe. This is such a lush, creamy, garlicky risotto that is made all that much better with a splash of wine for acidity and a subtle hint of prawn throughout. I highly recommend adding a sprinkle of crushed red pepper flakes and a rasp or two of lemon zest to round it all out. When you're done, you'll never order this out again knowing it cost you less than $3.00 a bowl!

COST PER SERVING: $2.23 | YIELD: 4 SERVINGS

6¼ cups (1.5 L) chicken stock

¼ cup (60 ml) extra virgin olive oil

1 yellow (brown) onion, peeled and diced

8 cloves garlic, roughly chopped

2 cups (400 g) uncooked arborio rice

⅓ cup (80 ml) dry white wine (optional)

12 prawns, peeled and raw

⅓ cup (20 g) parsley

Lemon zest, for serving

Crushed red pepper flakes, for serving

Salt and cracked black pepper, to taste

Add the stock to a saucepan and heat over low heat.

Add the olive oil to a different large saucepan and heat over medium heat. Sauté the onion for 5 minutes, or until it has softened. Add the garlic and cook for 2 minutes. Add the rice and toast it for 2 to 3 minutes before adding the wine (if using). Stir continuously for about 2 minutes, or until the wine has absorbed into the rice and the rice has thickened.

Add a ladle of stock to the rice, stirring constantly until the stock has been absorbed. Continue adding stock and stirring the rice until all of your stock has been used. With the last ladle of stock, add the prawns and parsley.

Continue stirring until the prawns are cooked (they will turn orange) and the rice is tender. You can add a little more stock if the rice isn't al dente by the time you've used it all. Serve in bowls with a generous zesting of lemon, red pepper flakes and salt and pepper, if needed.

GRILLED SARDINES WITH PARSLEY, LEMON ZEST AND TOMATO SEEDS ON CHARRED BREAD

Sardines are one of those fabulous Mediterranean staples that most people just don't seem to cook from scratch. I'm not sure why that's the case . . . maybe because sardines are so readily available canned from the supermarket. Or perhaps people think fresh sardines taste like they're canned from the supermarket!

Learning to cook sardines from scratch was a truly life-changing experience for me. Not only are they full of healthy fats and calcium (their bones are soft enough to chew), but they are spectacularly flavorful, affordable and pair beautifully with just about any herbs you have at home. This recipe is my favorite combination. The crisp, fresh and acidic flavors of parsley, lemon and tomato balance the buttery richness of hot grilled sardines perfectly. Keep the cooked sardines in the fridge for the next day if you have any leftovers.

COST PER SERVING: $1.77 | YIELD: 8 SERVINGS, AS A STARTER

18 oz (500 g) fresh sardines, headed and gutted

⅓ cup (80 ml) extra virgin olive oil, divided

Salt and cracked black pepper, to taste

2 stems Italian parsley, finely chopped

Zest of 1 lemon

1 tomato

8 slices of crusty bread (Vienna, *pane di casa* or your preferred loaf)

Heat a large nonstick griddle pan over medium heat. Add the sardines to your pan skin side down (if filleted) and drizzle with 2 tablespoons (30 ml) of the olive oil. Fry for 2 to 3 minutes, and carefully turn them over and fry for 2 to 3 minutes, or until each side has golden griddle lines. If you have whole sardines, fry them for 4 to 5 minutes on each side, as they'll be thicker and need a little longer to cook.

Carefully place the cooked sardines in a single layer on a serving plate, making sure to pour over any oils from the pan (that's the good stuff!). Sprinkle with salt, pepper and parsley, then zest a lemon over the sardines. Cut the tomato in half horizontally through the middle to expose the seeds. Gently squeeze the tomato halves over the plate, dressing the sardines with seeds. While the sardines are cooling slightly, toast the bread slices in the pan the sardines were just cooked in with your remaining olive oil. Cook each side for 2 to 3 minutes, or until they are beginning to char. Top each slice with sardines and dressing and enjoy.

BAKED FISH IN CARTOCCIO (PARCHMENT PAPER BAG)

Fish is a key ingredient in the Mediterranean diet, providing protein and healthy fats while being quite lean and very easy to cook. Cooking in cartoccio, a little paper bag that you fashion from parchment paper, is a surefire way to ensure your fish remains moist and flavorful while it's baking in the oven. It's a great way to start cooking fish as a beginner because even if you overcook it, it won't taste like you have!

COST PER SERVING: $2.05 | YIELD: 4 SERVINGS

4 (7-oz [200-g]) firm white fish fillets (blue grenadier, for example)

½ small fennel bulb, shaved or very finely sliced

3 tbsp (30 g) capers

⅔ cup (115 g) pitted green Sicilian olives, or any variety you love

Cracked black pepper, as needed

Extra virgin olive oil, as needed

Salt, as needed

Preheat the oven to 350°F (180°C).

Lay out each fish fillet onto the center of its own piece of parchment paper. Each piece of parchment should be at least 10 x 10 inches (25 x 25 cm) to ensure there's enough room for everything. Top each fillet equally with fennel, capers, olives, a few turns of the pepper mill and a drizzle of olive oil. Take the top and bottom of the parchment paper and fold together twice to form a seam. The paper should remain folded once you let go. Repeat the process with each side of the paper. You should now have a little paper bag with the fish inside it, and all the edges should be tightly folded so the juices don't seep out while cooking. Repeat this with the other pieces of fish.

Then place the paper bags onto a baking sheet and bake for 12 to 15 minutes. To check if they're fully cooked, cut a fillet in half. If the flesh is white rather than translucent, then the fish is done. If you have particularly thick pieces of fish, you may need to cook them a little longer. Serve in the paper bags with a sprinkle of salt if needed alongside my Garlicky Artichoke Salad (page 28) or Baked Zucchini with Pangrattato (page 31).

LEMON AND CAPER FISH PICCATA

You might've heard of piccata before. It's a dish that originated in Italy and can be made with any type of meat, although chicken is the most popular. While I love a classic, I adore this recipe with fish. These vibrant and zesty ingredients were made to be matched with white fish, and I just cannot get enough of it. Wholesome, fresh and packed with flavor and good-for-you fats, you can serve this with boiled or steamed potatoes, diced and dressed with a little vinegar, salt and olive oil, and you are set for an amazing meal.

COST PER SERVING: $1.91 | YIELD: 4 SERVINGS

⅓ cup (45 g) all-purpose flour

4 (7-oz [200-g]) firm white fish fillets (blue grenadier, for example)

¼ cup (60 ml) extra virgin olive oil, divided

4 cloves garlic, roughly chopped

½ cup (125 ml) dry white wine

1½ tbsp (16 g) chopped capers

1 tbsp (14 g) butter (optional)

Juice of 1 lemon

Salt, as needed

3 tbsp (10 g) chopped parsley

Place the flour in a shallow bowl or on a plate and add the fish fillets to the flour, one at a time. Coat both sides well and transfer to a clean plate.

Once all the fillets are floured, heat half of the olive oil in a large skillet. Add the fish fillets and gently lift them up with a spatula to help stop them from sticking. Then fry them without moving them again for 2 to 3 minutes, or until golden brown. Carefully turn the fish over and cook for another 2 minutes until golden.

Transfer the fish to a clean plate, then add the remaining olive oil and garlic to the pan. Cook for about 2 minutes, turning the heat down if needed so the garlic doesn't brown. Add the wine, capers and butter (if using) to the pan, swirling to pick up any browned bits that are stuck to the pan, and increase the heat to medium. When the butter has melted, add the fish fillets back to the pan along with any juices on the plate and cook until the sauce has thickened up to a gravy-like consistency, about 4 to 5 minutes. Squeeze the fresh lemon over the fillets, season with salt and top with parsley to serve.

BARBECUED OCTOPUS

You might've read at the start of the book about me falling head over heels in love for this simple-yet-impressive seafood snack. Each time I eat it, I imagine the fishermen hanging their octopus out to dry before cooking them fresh over smoking charcoal, the summer sun on my shoulders, the sea breeze . . . doesn't it just sound magical? This recipe will transport you to the European coastline in no time. Served with nothing more than a drizzle of the liquid gold that is antioxidant-rich extra virgin olive oil and some citrus and herbs, it's heaven for your body and your taste buds.

COST PER SERVING: $2.61 | YIELD: 4 SERVINGS, AS AN APERITIVO SNACK

FOR THE OCTOPUS

3 cloves garlic, bruised

1 lemon, halved

18 oz (500 g) octopus legs (approximately 5 legs—head and beak should already be removed)

FOR THE DRESSING

¼ cup (60 ml) extra virgin olive oil, plus extra for drizzling

¼ cup (16 g) chopped parsley

Juice of 1 lemon

1 clove garlic, finely chopped

½ tsp salt

¼ tsp cracked black pepper

To make the octopus, heat a large pot of water and add the garlic and lemon. Bring it to a full boil, then hold the octopus legs from their base with tongs and carefully and slowly dip the tentacles into the water three times, bringing them completely out each time. This helps to curl the tentacles. Then, boil the octopus for 45 to 50 minutes, and check that it is tender when pierced with a skewer. It shouldn't be too difficult to push a metal skewer the whole way through the thickest section. Once this is done, take the octopus out of the water and let it cool on a plate for 30 minutes.

While the octopus is cooling, make the dressing. Mix together the olive oil, parsley, lemon juice, garlic, salt and pepper in a small bowl. After 20 minutes you can cut up the octopus into individual legs. Heat your barbecue grill up nice and hot, drizzle the octopus legs with a little olive oil, and place them on the grill for a couple of minutes each side until they are charred. Slice the legs into bite-size pieces and spoon the dressing over them. Serve while hot. For serving, I like to put toothpicks into each piece of octopus for easy eating.

My Favorite
CHICKEN RECIPES

I'll hazard a guess and say chicken is the most commonly consumed meat in Australia. As we are a country built by immigrants, we have the unique opportunity to experience and be exposed to recipes including chicken from all different cultures and cuisines. Many of these include Mediterranean recipes, thanks to the assisted passage of European and Turkish migrants from the post–World War II era through to the '70s. So there's really no surprise that it's so incredibly popular.

Chicken and poultry are situated near the top of the Mediterranean food pyramid, meaning that it can be enjoyed as part of a traditional Mediterranean diet, but just on occasion. I usually keep chicken dishes to a once-per-week occurrence and opt for vegetarian and seafood meals the other nights of the week. Because chicken is usually quite lean and very affordable compared to other meat, it's a great option to include in a budget-friendly menu. It's also a wonderful conveyor of flavor, taking on whatever you cook it with, so even the fussiest eaters can enjoy chicken.

A couple of years ago, I visited Parma in Italy. I traveled alone as I often do for work, and one of my favorite things to do is take myself out to dinner. This night I wandered into a gorgeous trattoria and ordered their chicken cacciatore, which featured a gloriously golden, crispy-skinned piece of chicken swimming in a pool of dark tomato *sugo*, dotted with forest-fresh mushrooms and deep green olives. I always take notes when I go out to eat, and once I got home, I began working on a quick and easy version of this beautiful classic. The trick, the waiter told me, was a few anchovies in the sauce. Although you can't see or taste them, they add a rich saltiness that would be missing otherwise.

Along with my version of that incredible Parma trattoria Green Olive Chicken Cacciatore (page 92), I've added to this chapter an amazing Cozy Chicken Marbella (page 91), which is a one-pan wonder, and BBQ Lemon and Herb Chicken (page 95) tenderized in yogurt and lemon. And I just know that they will become favorites in your home, just the way they have become favorites in mine.

ONE-PAN ROAST CHICKEN

Everyone loves an easy, straightforward dinner, and this dish is exactly that. The bold flavors in this dish are just so satisfying. Think lots of olive oil and tomato baked down into a delicious, rich *sugo* (sauce), dotted with olives that hug each potato and perfectly complement the crispy-skinned roast chicken on top (which then soaks up all the sauce—yum!). You can easily double the potatoes, tomatoes and olives to provide a fabulous lunch for the next day as well, which I highly recommend, and still come in under budget!

COST PER SERVING: $1.87 | YIELD: 4 SERVINGS

4 potatoes (approximately 28 oz [800 g]), skin on, diced into small pieces

¾ cup (130 g) pitted kalamata olives

1 (14-oz [400-g]) can crushed tomatoes

1 whole butterflied chicken (approximately 2 lbs [1 kg])

Salt and cracked black pepper, as needed

4 sprigs thyme, leaves removed

¼ cup (60 ml) extra virgin olive oil

Preheat the oven to 350°F (180°C).

Place the potatoes into a large, heavy baking dish, spreading them out evenly so they're more or less in a nice, even layer. Add the olives and crushed tomatoes over the top of them, flattening them down into an even layer. Place the butterflied chicken on top and season it with a generous pinch of salt, pepper, thyme leaves and olive oil drizzled over the whole dish.

Roast for about 50 minutes, or until the chicken is cooked through. You can check this with a meat thermometer by putting it into the center of the thickest part of the chicken. You know it's ready when the temperature is above 165°F (75°C).

Rest the whole dish for 5 minutes before slicing the chicken into four pieces (Marylands and breasts) and serving with plenty of vegetables and sauce.

COZY CHICKEN MARBELLA

Now, this is definitely not a traditional Mediterranean recipe. It actually originated in New York as an Italian/Jewish hybrid recipe. However, the mainstays of the original recipe are quintessentially Mediterranean and full of flavor, so although it's not traditional, I knew I had to include it because it still speaks to the heart of Mediterranean cooking. I've tweaked and changed this recipe around quite a bit for my own preferences, making it less sweet, with a cheaper cut of chicken and an easier cooking method so you can still enjoy it on a regular basis. Although it might be tempting to shorten the marinade time, it's important that you let it marinate overnight because this process tenderizes the chicken and allows the skins to really crisp up once cooked.

COST PER SERVING: $1.58 | YIELD: 4 SERVINGS

8 chicken drumsticks

1 cup (180 g) pitted prunes

⅔ cup (115 g) Sicilian green olives (or your favorite variety)

3½ tbsp (35 g) capers

8 cloves garlic, peeled and bruised

6 bay leaves

⅓ cup (80 ml) extra virgin olive oil

⅓ cup (80 ml) red wine vinegar

2 tsp (12 g) salt

1 tsp cracked black pepper

¾ cup (185 ml) dry white wine

1 heaping tbsp (13 g) brown sugar

Roasted or steamed potatoes, for serving

Layer the drumsticks into a large shallow baking dish. Add the prunes, olives, capers, garlic and bay leaves, making sure you push them down into the dish and wedge them in between the chicken. Pour the olive oil and red wine vinegar over the dish and season with salt and pepper. Put a lid on the baking dish and let it marinate in the fridge overnight.

Preheat the oven to 350°F (180°C).

Take the dish from the fridge and, using tongs, turn each drumstick over. Add the wine and evenly sprinkle the brown sugar over the top. Bake with the lid off for 45 minutes, then increase the oven temperature to 425°F (220°C) for 12 to 15 minutes. Let the chicken rest for 5 minutes before serving with some roasted or steamed potatoes.

GREEN OLIVE CHICKEN CACCIATORE

Chicken cacciatore, or "hunter's chicken," is an old Italian recipe that I really only started eating once it was recommended to me in Parma. We never had it growing up because my dad doesn't like olives (not a very good Italian, eh?), but I have certainly made up for it now. I make my cacciatore with green olives, because they are a little subtler in flavor, and I love that at any given time, I have the majority of ingredients ready to go in my pantry. You can use any cut of chicken you like best, but bone-in chicken thighs make it thrifty, and I do love chicken on the bone. It has so much more flavor! If you really want to take this recipe to the next level, add in two anchovy fillets with the tomatoes. Trust me (or should I say, trust the waiter I had in Parma!).

COST PER SERVING: $2.80 | YIELD: 4 SERVINGS

¼ cup (60 ml) extra virgin olive oil

1 yellow (brown) onion, peeled and sliced

4 bone-in chicken thighs (chops) (approximately 1½ lbs [700 g])

3 cups (200 g) button mushrooms, halved or quartered, to your preference

3 cloves garlic, roughly chopped

1 tsp dried rosemary

1 (14-oz [400-g]) can crushed tomatoes

Salt and cracked black pepper, as needed

⅓ cup (60 g) pitted Sicilian green olives

Crusty bread, for serving (optional)

Heat a shallow saucepan over medium heat before drizzling in the olive oil and adding the onion. Sauté for 5 minutes, or until it begins to soften. Create some space for the chicken and add each piece, skin-side down. Fry the chicken pieces for 4 to 5 minutes, or until the skin has browned. Then turn them over and add the mushrooms, garlic and rosemary.

Cook for 5 minutes, stirring occasionally. Add the tomatoes and season with salt and pepper. Reduce the heat to low and simmer for about 25 minutes. Add the olives and stir for a few minutes before serving as is, or with crusty bread if desired.

BBQ LEMON AND HERB CHICKEN

Whenever I think of Greece, I think of charcoal pits cooking perfectly seasoned lamb, chicken and fish like my friends used to cook in their backyard for Orthodox Easter. The yogurt in this recipe is key. It works as a tenderizer and marinade, and when combined with garlic and lemon, it is simply stunning. You can bake this dish in the oven or fry it in a pan if you don't have a barbecue grill or charcoal pit (I wouldn't think many of us do!), and the result is still mouthwatering.

COST PER SERVING: $1.12 | YIELD: 4 SERVINGS

18 oz (500 g) chicken thighs or chicken breast cut into vertical strips, about 1–1½ inch (3–4 cm) wide

⅓ cup (100 g) Greek yogurt

6 cloves garlic, roughly chopped

3 sprigs thyme, leaves removed

2½ tbsp (40 ml) extra virgin olive oil

Juice of 1 lemon

¼ tsp cracked black pepper

½ tsp salt

Place the chicken, yogurt, garlic, thyme, olive oil, lemon juice, pepper and salt in a large bowl and combine well with a spoon. Cover the bowl and let the marinade thicken for at least 1 hour or overnight.

When you're ready to cook, get your grill nice and hot, and cook the chicken for 4 to 5 minutes on each side, or until browned and cooked through. Serve the chicken while it's hot with my Orzo Salad with Cucumber, Tomato and Basil (page 57) or Shepherd's Salad with White Beans (page 53).

TURKISH-STYLE CHICKEN KEBABS

In Turkey, I had chicken shish kebabs that were cooked with a mixture of herbs, spices, citrus and red pepper paste called *biber salçasi*. This isn't a very common ingredient, so I make it at home with tomato paste and smoked paprika, and it really hits the spot. These are best cooked on a barbecue grill for that extra bit of deliciousness.

COST PER KEBAB: $0.48 | YIELD: 8 KEBABS

2 chicken breasts (14 oz [400 g]), evenly diced into 1-inch (3-cm) squares

3 tbsp (48 g) tomato paste

½ tsp salt

1 tbsp (7 g) smoked paprika

1 tsp cumin

¼ tsp cayenne pepper (optional)

½ tsp cracked black pepper

Juice of ½ lemon

1 large red onion, peeled and quartered

1 large green bell pepper (capsicum), deseeded and chopped into ¾ x ¾-inch (2 x 2–cm) pieces

Wooden skewers, soaked in water prior to using and cooking

Place the chicken in a large bowl along with the tomato paste, salt, paprika, cumin, cayenne pepper (if using), black pepper and lemon juice. Combine really well and cover the bowl. You can marinate this anywhere from 1 hour to overnight.

Carefully thread pieces of chicken, thin pieces of onion and chunks of bell pepper onto the skewers until you've used all your ingredients. Make sure the skewers are not too tightly packed as they will take longer to cook. You can grill the skewers either on a barbecue grill or in a nonstick skillet on medium high heat with a splash of olive oil. Turn the skewers every few minutes until the chicken has browned and cooked through, approximately 15 minutes. Serve right away.

Braised,
BAKED AND BARBECUED:
MEDITERRANEAN MEAT DISHES

In Mediterranean cuisine, red meat has traditionally been reserved for celebrations and special occasions. Lamb and beef have always been luxurious ingredients, and while today we might consume them more often than our ancestors did, they are still quite expensive, especially when compared to protein-rich legumes. Cooking on a budget does not need to mean cooking without flavor, especially when it comes to meat.

Lamb and beef mince are very economical, and they are also quite versatile. They have hundreds of applications, and I use them regularly to make Bulgur and Lamb Kofta (page 104) and fragrant Smoky Stuffed Peppers with Lamb (page 108). Another great option for cooking meat on a budget is using good quality sausages, which are already packed with flavor and seasoning. Squeeze them out of their casings, fry off the chunks until golden and you have the base to a mouthwatering pasta sauce. I tell you how to make my Italian Pork Sausage and Sage Rigatoni (page 100) using this method.

I will also show you my favorite BBQ pork recipe (BBQ Pork Chop with Sage [page 111]) that makes me nostalgic for Easter and Christmas with my family every time I smell the simple-but-tasty sage marinade. In this chapter, I tell you that you can still enjoy meat, just in smaller quantities to keep the grocery budget in check.

ITALIAN PORK SAUSAGE AND SAGE RIGATONI

Five ingredients and a whole lot of flavor. This is such an easy, fuss-free recipe that can be ready in no time at all. The first time I ate a dish similar to this was in the Roman neighborhood of Trastevere. There, I sampled fennel and pork sausage fried up in olive oil with a splash of wine. It was beyond amazing, and during aperitivo that evening, I noted down a rough recipe in my notebook. Upon returning home, I began making it myself. I really like adding tomatoes because they cut through the richness of the pork so wonderfully and add a little more coating over each piece of pasta.

COST PER SERVING: $1.10 | YIELD: 4 SERVINGS

2½ tbsp (40 ml) extra virgin olive oil

3 large good quality pork sausages (approximately 9 oz [250 g])

1⅔ cups (250 g) cherry tomatoes

10 sage leaves, finely sliced

12 oz (340 g) rigatoni

Salt and cracked black pepper, to taste

Heat a pot of salted water until it's boiling. While it's heating up, add the olive oil to a skillet over medium heat. Squeeze the sausage meat out of the sausage casing straight into the skillet, and add the cherry tomatoes and sage. Use a wooden spoon to break up the sausage meat into chunks.

Cook the sausage for 8 to 10 minutes, or until the tomatoes are soft and saucy and the meat has cooked through, stirring occasionally. If the sauce gets a little too thick, you can add some of the pasta water to thin it out again.

Once the water boils, add the rigatoni and cook it until it's al dente. Scoop the pasta out with a slotted spoon, and add it to the sauce while it's still in the pan. Stir to let the rigatoni soak up some sauce, season to taste and serve straight away.

EGGPLANT AND BEEF MOUSSAKA

This is a traditional Greek recipe and one of the first recipes I had to make in food science class while at university. I'd never tried moussaka before that kitchen practical, let alone made it, but it reminded me of lasagna, just without the pasta. The one thing I remember was my good friend Sarah and I discussing how much we loved the addition of cinnamon to the sauce. It changed the whole dish from what felt to me at the time like a very Italian recipe to something completely new. This meal is one of my favorites in the whole book. So, if I were you, I'd make double, because this will get cleaned up!

COST PER SERVING: $2.32 | YIELD: 4 SERVINGS

FOR THE EGGPLANT

3 large eggplants (approximately 2 lbs [1 kg])

1 tsp salt

Extra virgin olive oil, for drizzling

1 cup (100 g) grated mozzarella

FOR THE SAUCE

¼ cup (60 ml) extra virgin olive oil

1 yellow (brown) onion, finely sliced

9 oz (250 g) ground beef

4 cloves garlic, finely chopped

½ tsp cinnamon

½ tsp salt

¼ tsp cracked black pepper

1 (14-oz [400-g]) can crushed tomatoes

1 heaping tbsp (16 g) tomato paste

Preheat the oven to 350°F (180°C).

To make the eggplant, slice the eggplants lengthways into ½-inch (1.25-cm)-thick slices, discarding the stalks. Place the slices onto parchment-lined baking sheets, season with the salt and drizzle with olive oil. Bake for 15 to 20 minutes, or until softened and beginning to brown.

While the eggplant is baking, make the sauce. Heat the olive oil in a large skillet and add the onion. Sauté for 5 minutes, then add the ground beef and break it up with a wooden spoon. Add the garlic, cinnamon, salt and pepper. Cook and stir for about 10 minutes, or until the mince has browned and the mixture is quite dry. Add the crushed tomatoes and tomato paste, reduce the heat to low and simmer for 15 minutes.

¼ cup (60 ml) extra virgin olive oil

⅓ cup (45 g) all-purpose flour

2 cups (500 ml) milk

¼ tsp salt

¼ tsp cracked black pepper

¼ tsp nutmeg

¼ cup (25 g) grated Parmesan

While the sauce is simmering, make the béchamel. Heat the olive oil in a saucepan over medium heat. Add the flour and cook, stirring with a wooden spoon, for 1 minute. It will become very thick. Gradually stir in the milk, about ½ cup (125 ml) at a time, mixing well to stir out any lumps and letting the mixture thicken before adding in more milk. Repeat this step until you've added all of the milk. Stir in the salt, pepper, nutmeg and Parmesan and cook and stir for 4 to 5 minutes, or until the béchamel thickens. The consistency should be like thin pancake batter. Take the béchamel off the heat.

Once the sauce is done, you're ready to assemble the moussaka. Place a few spoonfuls of sauce in the bottom of a 8-inch (22-cm) round baking dish and add a single layer of eggplant on top. The eggplant should be soft so you can squeeze in extra pieces to make sure you have completely covered the sauce. Add a thick layer of sauce on top. Then add the béchamel and another layer of eggplant. Repeat this until you've used all your ingredients. I always have three layers of eggplant, sauce and béchamel.

Top with the mozzarella, and bake for 30 minutes, or until the cheese is golden. Let the moussaka rest for 5 minutes before slicing and serving.

*See image on page 98.

BULGUR AND LAMB KOFTA

Koftas are a feature of many Greek and Turkish menus, and with good reason. They are universally loved for their incredible taste and mouthfeel. It's also a popular recipe to make because you can enrich it with any herbs or spices you might have on hand. This recipe is my favorite way to eat kofta, even if it's a little unorthodox since it's heavy on the bulgur, which is wonderfully chewy and lowers the cost per serving substantially. If you don't have sumac in your pantry, just add some lemon zest instead.

COST PER SERVING: $0.75 | YIELD: 4 SERVINGS

1 cup (140 g) fine bulgur

9 oz (250 g) ground lamb

2 tsp (2 g) dried mint

1 tsp dried oregano

1 tsp sumac

2 tsp (4 g) smoked paprika

2 tsp (4 g) cumin

1 tsp salt, plus extra as needed

1 egg

½ cup (55 g) breadcrumbs

Extra virgin olive oil (optional)

Greek yogurt, for serving

Fresh lemon juice, to taste

Place the bulgur into a heatproof bowl and cover it with boiling water. Place a plate on top and let it soak for 10 minutes. Drain the bulgur in a colander and let it cool for a few minutes.

Add the ground lamb, mint, oregano, sumac, paprika, cumin, salt, egg, breadcrumbs and cooled (to the touch) bulgur to a large bowl. Mix together with your hands (this is the easiest way). Once it's well combined, shape equal portions into long meatball or kofta shapes. You can set them aside onto a plate, or you can place them straight into a large nonstick frying pan over medium heat and cook as you go. Depending on your pan, you might need to add a drizzle of olive oil.

Turn the koftas until they are cooked through and browned on all sides, about 12 to 15 minutes. Serve hot with some Greek yogurt, a sprinkle of salt and a squeeze of fresh lemon.

LAMB, CHICKPEA AND YOGURT STEW

When I was testing this recipe for the book, my neighbor Simon commented that it was like comfort in a container, and he wasn't wrong. It blends Greek and Turkish flavors to create a beautiful mix of lamb, garlic, chickpeas and yogurt, and the taste is phenomenal. Once again, the yogurt is tenderizing and tart, which just cuts so brilliantly through the ground lamb, which is quite fatty and rich (as it should be). Serve this over rice, with potatoes or with crusty toasted bread.

COST PER SERVING: $1.72 | YIELD: 4 SERVINGS

¼ cup (60 ml) extra virgin olive oil

1 yellow (brown) onion, finely diced

4 cloves garlic, roughly chopped

18 oz (500 g) ground lamb

1 (14-oz [400-g]) can chickpeas, drained and rinsed

1 tsp salt

½ tsp cracked black pepper

1 tsp dried mint

1¼ cups (350 g) Greek yogurt

1¼ cups (300 ml) water

1 tsp corn flour

Cooked rice, potatoes or toasted bread, for serving (optional)

Heat the olive oil in a large, heavy saucepan over medium heat. Add the onion and garlic and sauté for 5 minutes. Add the lamb and chickpeas and cook for 10 minutes. Once the lamb has browned and cooked through, stir in the salt, pepper and dried mint, then take it off the heat. Let it cool for at least 10 minutes, stirring every minute or so to help it cool down.

While the lamb is cooling, combine the yogurt, water and corn flour in a small saucepan over very low heat. Mix with a whisk once to smooth out the corn flour, then let it cook on very low heat for 10 minutes. After the lamb has cooled for 10 or so minutes, slowly pour the yogurt into the mince and combine. Serve by itself or with some rice, potatoes or toasted bread.

SMOKY STUFFED PEPPERS WITH LAMB

There are versions of the Greek *yemista*, or "stuffed vegetables," throughout the Mediterranean. They range from bell peppers (capsicums) and tomatoes to eggplants and zucchini. All are traditionally filled with a rice mixture that can be enhanced with a little ground lamb or beef and plenty of herbs and spices. Unbelievably delicious, and it's inexpensive to make, even if you find yourself cooking for a crowd.

COST PER SERVING: $1.74 | YIELD: 4 SERVINGS

¼ cup (60 ml) extra virgin olive oil

1 red onion, finely diced

4 cloves garlic, finely chopped

4 oz (100 g) ground lamb

1 heaping tsp smoked paprika

1 (14-oz [400-g]) can crushed tomatoes

1 cup (200 g) uncooked long grain white rice

1 tsp salt, plus extra for seasoning

½ tsp cracked black pepper, plus extra for seasoning

3 tbsp (10 g) roughly torn parsley

4 red bell peppers (capsicums), hollowed out

Preheat the oven to 350°F (180°C) .

Heat the olive oil in a large skillet over medium heat. Add the onion and garlic and sauté for 5 minutes. Add the ground lamb and cook for 4 to 5 minutes, or until browned, while breaking up the ground lamb with a wooden spoon.

Add the paprika and mix, then pour in the crushed tomatoes straight from the can. Fill the can three-quarters full with water and add that to the pan. Add the rice, salt, pepper and parsley and stir.

Reduce the heat to low, and simmer for 15 minutes, or until the moisture has absorbed and the rice is tender. Take the rice off the heat and cool for 5 minutes.

Carefully stuff each bell pepper full of the rice mixture and place them onto a baking sheet. Once all the peppers are filled, bake for 25 to 30 minutes, or until the peppers are tender. Season to taste and serve.

BBQ PORK CHOP WITH SAGE

This recipe reminds me of my dad and nonno standing at the barbecue cooking lunch at Christmas or Easter time, whether it's rain, hail or shine. My nonna would marinate all the chicken and pork in an abundance of homegrown sage, salt and a generous pour of olive oil, and then hand it to my dad to take outside to cook. It's a simple combination that works so perfectly altogether.

COST PER SERVING: $1.43 | YIELD: 4 SERVINGS

4 pork chops (approximately 1½ lbs [700 g])

¼ cup (60 ml) extra virgin olive oil

10 sage leaves, torn

1½ tsp (9 g) salt

1 tsp cracked black pepper

Place the pork chops in a large bowl, drizzle the olive oil over them and add the sage, salt and pepper. Use your hands to mix around and coat the pork in everything. You can marinate this anywhere from 20 minutes to overnight covered or in a closed container.

When you're ready to cook, get the barbecue grill nice and hot. If you have a thermometer available, aim for 400°F (200°C). Mix the pork chops around again to recoat each piece in marinade and, using tongs, place them onto the BBQ grill. Cook each side for 3 to 4 minutes, or until you have dark char lines and the pork is cooked through. Serve straight from the grill with any of the salads from the Hearty Wholesome Vegetables chapter (page 11).

Good-for-You
(AND YOUR WALLET) SAUCES, SPREADS AND DIPS

When I was growing up, "fast food" came in the form of pasta and a jar of sauce from the fridge or freezer. My mum would make a big batch of sauce and divide it up into a few portions so she could organize dinner in a jiffy and on a budget.

Sauces, spreads and dips are normally an afterthought—not exactly the main event when making a meal—but I promise you that this chapter will have you seeing them as stars of the show. A punchy, vibrant, aromatic sauce can elevate an average plate of pasta to lofty heights, providing a new sensation and discovery with every bite and fireworks as you bite into something new. And, best of all, you'll get that immense feeling of accomplishment when you find a table full of empty plates.

Some recipes are fast—60 seconds and you're done—like with my Rustic Walnut Pesto (page 121) or White Bean Hummus (page 129). And others are a slow burn, like My Favorite Bolognese (page 114) or fire-roasted Smoky Bell Pepper Sauce (page 118). But a slow sauce is my personal favorite. You get to enjoy the process of preparing each step and then savoring the intoxicating fragrance that will drift from the pot throughout the kitchen and into the rest of the house. Nothing beats smelling what's cooking while walking up to your front door.

By batch cooking and freezing, you will not only have convenience but also less waste and a lower cost per serving. These recipes are also a wonderfully simple way to increase your and your family's vegetable intake. Getting those five servings has never been easier when you're enjoying them on crackers as a snack, loaded up on sandwiches for lunch, drizzled over salads as a dressing and stirred through pasta for dinner.

MY FAVORITE BOLOGNESE

Bolognese sauce is one of those sauces that should always be in everyone's fridge or freezer. There's nothing better than taking a tub of thick, rich and comforting Bolognese from the freezer and quickly heating it up in a pot while your pasta water boils, and then serving it piping hot loaded up with Parmesan. Tomatoes and milk are actually the key ingredients here and not only are they cheap, but they're also pretty much available in any pantry you peek into. This is also a fab recipe to double if you want to stock up your freezer or prepare a lasagna or two!

COST PER SERVING: $0.91 | YIELD: 6 SERVINGS

⅓ cup (80 ml) extra virgin olive oil

1 yellow (brown) onion, peeled and diced

2 celery ribs, leaves removed and diced

1 large carrot, skin on and diced

18 oz (500 g) ground beef

¾ cup (180 ml) dry white wine

1¼ (18-oz [500-g]) cans crushed tomatoes

1 cup (250 ml) milk

¼ tsp nutmeg, plus extra as needed

½ tsp salt, plus extra as needed

Heat the olive oil in a heavy saucepan over medium heat, and add the onion, celery and carrot. Sauté for about 15 minutes, or until the onion is translucent.

Add the beef and stir to break it up every minute or so for just under 10 minutes, until the beef is browned. Add the white wine and cook and stir for 2 minutes to pick up any caramelization in your saucepan (this is flavor!).

Add the tomatoes, milk, nutmeg and salt and simmer on low for at least 1 hour and up to 2 hours. You'll know it's ready when the oil has settled on top of the saucepan and the sauce has thickened. Adjust the seasoning to taste, and serve with your favorite pasta, or freeze for later use.

PUTTANESCA SAUCE

This sauce's namesake has some interesting beginnings that I've always loved learning about. "Puttanesca" comes from the Italian word *puttanata*, which basically means "worthless." However, I think this recipe is more priceless than anything else because it's so inexpensive to make, and it satisfies time and time again with its big, bold, punchy and bright flavors. I'd like to note that this recipe uses two anchovies, and I know they're not everyone's cup of tea, but please trust me and try it. They melt into nothing and add such an incredible layer of flavor that is not fishy in the slightest.

COST PER SERVING: $0.42 | YIELD: 4 SERVINGS

⅓ cup (80 ml) extra virgin olive oil

4 cloves garlic, roughly chopped

¼ cup (40 g) capers

Heaping ⅓ cup (70 g) pitted kalamata olives

1 (14-oz [400-g]) can crushed tomatoes

2 anchovy fillets from a jar (optional, but seriously amazing)

½ tsp chili paste

Heat the olive oil in a large saucepan over medium-low heat. Add the garlic and capers, and cook for about 10 minutes. You want the garlic to become slightly translucent and tender and the capers to relax and open up a little. Be careful to reduce the heat if the garlic begins to brown.

Add the olives and cook for 1 minute or so, or until fragrant. Pour in the tomatoes and refill the tomato can with water until half full. Add this to the saucepan along with the anchovies and chili paste.

Simmer over low heat for 45 minutes, or until the sauce is thick and the oil has floated to the top. You can serve it right away or freeze in batches for a quick-and-easy pasta dinner.

SMOKY BELL PEPPER SAUCE

Bell peppers (capsicums) are one of those things I never really learned to appreciate until I began traveling. As soon as I hit the Mediterranean during the summer of 2011, I saw them everywhere. In *pepperonata* in Italy, *ajvar* in Croatia and in sauces, salads and sides everywhere. I loved how sweet and tender they were after grilling them whole over a barbecue grill and would save any charred pieces as the last thing I ate off my plate. So, this sauce is a culmination of all the things I loved about my first Mediterranean summer, which was done on a tight budget, just like this recipe!

COST PER SERVING: $1.11 | YIELD: 4 SERVINGS, AS A PASTA SAUCE, OR 1 LARGE JAR

3 large red bell peppers (capsicums)

⅓ cup (80 ml) extra virgin olive oil

3 cloves garlic, roughly chopped

½–1 tsp chili paste (depending on taste)

4 tbsp (65 g) tomato paste

½ tsp smoked paprika

1 (14-oz [400-g]) can crushed tomatoes

1 heaping tsp brown sugar

1½ tsp (9 g) salt, plus extra to taste

Turn the gas of one of your burners to medium heat, and carefully place a bell pepper directly over the flame using metal tongs. If you don't have a gas burner, you can use a cooking torch. The flame will begin to blister and burn the pepper skin, and this is exactly what we want. Once the skin has blackened, carefully turn the pepper, repeating until the entire pepper has black skin. Place the charred pepper into a large bowl and cover it with a plate to sweat. Char the remaining peppers and pop them into the bowl to sweat as well for about 20 minutes. Peel the charred peppers over the sink. Place the blackened skins into the bowl and the soft, tender grilled peppers onto a clean plate. Pull the stalk and seeds out while you're peeling them and discard. If the charred skin is sticking a little bit, turn the tap on and rinse the pepper while peeling.

Once all the bell peppers are peeled, slice them into rounds and add to a large saucepan along with the olive oil. Heat over medium heat. Add the garlic, chili paste, tomato paste and paprika and sauté for 2 to 3 minutes. Add the tomatoes and fill the tomato can one-third full with water, and add that in along with the brown sugar and salt. Reduce the heat to the lowest it can go to, and simmer for at least 1 hour and up to 2 hours. Season to taste or add a little more chili if you like it, and serve with your favorite pasta, on top of sausages or with BBQ Lemon and Herb Chicken (page 95).

RUSTIC WALNUT PESTO

I'll eat pesto any which way, but I have to say this is my favorite. I love highlighting the delicious texture of walnuts, and it doesn't hurt that they're far more affordable than the pine nuts in traditional pesto. Plus, they're loaded with healthy unsaturated fats. Teamed up with gorgeously bright and fresh lemon and basil, this becomes a wonderful pesto for pasta, risotto, salads and over roasted potatoes or even with some cheese on bruschetta.

COST PER SERVING: $0.34 | YIELD: 1 GENEROUS CUP, AS A PASTA SAUCE

½ cup (60 g) walnuts

1½ cups (30 g) basil leaves

Zest of 1 lemon

½ tsp salt

½ tsp cracked black pepper

¼ cup (60 ml) extra virgin olive oil

This is a recipe that you can make either in a food processor or in a mortar and pestle.

If using a food processor, add the walnuts, basil, lemon zest, salt, pepper and olive oil and pulse until combined.

If using a mortar and pestle, gently crush the walnuts into small pieces, then add the basil leaves and begin to work them into the walnuts until they are broken down into a rustic puree. Add the lemon zest, salt and pepper, and combine again. With a spoon, scrape any pesto off the pestle and gently stir in the olive oil.

Serve on Ricotta Gnocchi (page 37) or store in the fridge as a dressing or pizza base.

THREE GREENS PESTO

The best thing about this recipe is that you can use any greens you have at home. Arugula, basil and parsley are the greens I usually have growing on my balcony, but you can get creative and use carrot tops, spinach or even beet leaves. No matter the combination, it's always bursting with freshness and flavor. The recipe makes one large jar, and you can store it in the fridge for up to a week to use in pasta, Pesto Risotto (page 42), on salads and as a bruschetta topping.

COST PER JAR: $1.75 | YIELD: 1 GENEROUS CUP

⅓ cup (6 g) arugula

1 cup (20 g) basil

¼ cup (16 g) parsley

½ cup (50 g) grated Parmesan

½ cup (125 ml) extra virgin olive oil

Juice of ½ lemon

1 cup (125 g) walnuts

1 clove garlic, peeled

¼ tsp cracked black pepper

¼–½ tsp salt

Place the arugula, basil, parsley, Parmesan, olive oil, lemon juice, walnuts, garlic, pepper and salt into a food processor and pulse until blended to your desired consistency.

I like this pesto a little chunky for some texture, but if I'm using it for sandwiches or as a pizza base, I make it smooth like sauce so it's easier to spread.

BROCCOLI AND ALMOND PESTO

While pesto is usually made with herbs or a variety of greens (like with my Three Greens Pesto [page 122]), you can also use veggies to change it up! Use fresh broccoli if it's in season, otherwise head to the freezer section at your local supermarket and pick up some frozen broccoli. It works just as well and is usually a fraction of the price of fresh broccoli!

COST PER JAR: $1.39 | YIELD: 1 LARGE JAR

2¼ cups (200 g) broccoli stalks and florets, fresh or frozen

⅓ cup (45 g) roasted almonds

1½ tbsp (16 g) capers

½ cup (125 ml) extra virgin olive oil

¼ tsp cracked black pepper, plus extra as needed

1 clove garlic

Juice of ½ lemon

½ tsp salt, plus extra as needed

Place the broccoli in a steaming basket over a pot of boiling water for 7 to 8 minutes, or until the broccoli turns vibrant green in color and is tender when you insert a knife or skewer.

Dry the steamed broccoli with paper towels and let the broccoli cool for 10 minutes, and place in a food processor. Add the almonds, capers, olive oil, pepper, garlic, lemon juice and salt, and pulse until combined well but still a little chunky. Adjust the seasoning if you feel it needs it, and serve with crusty toasted bread, over pasta or on chicken sandwiches.

PUMPKIN AND FETA DIP

This is such a fabulously cost-effective and filling dip. You can use any pumpkin you like, either your favorite variety or whatever is cheapest when grocery shopping, because all the flavor comes from roasting the pumpkin with salt, olive oil and garlic. The smell that floats through the kitchen while this is baking is mouthwatering all on its own!

COST PER SERVING: $0.25 | YIELD: 8 SERVINGS, AS A DIP

14 oz (400 g) pumpkin, any variety

4 cloves garlic, whole and peeled

1 tsp salt, plus extra to taste

¼ cup (60 ml) extra virgin olive oil, plus extra as needed

1 (14-oz [400-g]) can chickpeas, drained and rinsed

⅔ cup (100 g) feta cheese

Toasted pine nuts (optional)

Preheat the oven to 350°F (180°C).

Peel the pumpkin and remove the seeds if there are any. I like to peel pumpkins with a vegetable peeler, as it's much quicker and easier than using a knife. Cut the pumpkin into slices, then dice into 1 x 1–inch (3 x 3–cm) pieces. Place onto a parchment-lined baking sheet in an even layer. Add the garlic, sprinkle with salt, then drizzle with olive oil. Roast for 25 to 30 minutes, or until the pumpkin is golden.

Cool the pumpkin and garlic for 15 minutes, then add them to a food processor along with the chickpeas and feta. Process until the dip is smooth and combined. Adjust seasoning if needed, and serve with a drizzle of olive oil and even a spoonful of toasted pine nuts if you have them on hand.

WHITE BEAN HUMMUS

Hummus is such a cheap and cheerful staple in my fridge. We eat it on toast, in wraps, as a dip and even layered on grilled lamb and salad. The options are endless! I learned how to make the best hummus I've ever had from a taxi driver in Tel Aviv. He was driving me to the Levinsky Market, where I'd hoped to find some spices and tahini to bring home to Australia. He told me which tahini to buy, how to keep it pale and white (rather than brown) while making hummus, and then explained the method that his father taught him when he was a boy. I quickly noted everything down in my phone notes while we weaved through traffic. And I underlined the most important step: Use ice cubes rather than water. I changed up the traditional recipe to use white beans, which blend into a gorgeous creamy texture and are something I always have on hand in my pantry.

COST PER BOWL: $1.86 | YIELD: 1 LARGE BOWL

1 (14-oz [400-g]) can white lima beans

2½ tbsp (40 ml) brine from the bean can

¼ cup + 1 tbsp (80 g) hulled tahini

⅓ cup (80 ml) extra virgin olive oil, plus extra for serving

Zest of 1 lemon

Juice of ½ lemon

1 clove garlic, minced

1 tsp sea salt flakes

2 ice cubes

Fresh parsley (optional)

Cracked black pepper (optional)

Drain the beans in a colander, reserving the liquid, and rinse the beans with water and dry them off on a paper towel.

Place the beans, reserved liquid, tahini, olive oil, lemon zest, lemon juice, garlic and salt in a food processor with the ice cubes on top. Let the ice cubes melt completely, and process until your hummus is smooth and creamy. You might like to add a little more olive oil for a thinner hummus.

Serve with some fresh parsley, cracked black pepper and a drizzle of olive oil on top.

A SWEET NOTE TO FINISH ON

Desserts are not the main attraction of Mediterranean cuisine. Unlike other European cuisines, the desserts throughout the region favor lighter, fresher ingredients rather than buttery pastries and chocolate—but don't worry, they're equally enticing and delicious!

As I briefly touched on earlier, the evening meal in Italy often begins early with an aperitivo or snack accompanied by a cocktail or drink. Then dinner is a three-course affair starting with antipasto (usually a mix of cured and pickled vegetables with cold cuts and bread) before moving onto the *primo piatto* (a first plate of pasta or risotto) and *secondo piatto* (a second plate usually of meat). All of this is paired with a carafe or bottle of wine, so by the time coffee and dessert rolls around, you really need something light, bright and punchy to end the meal.

Dessert for me has never been a struggle. I absolutely love sweets no matter how full I am, and they do say that dessert has its own stomach for a reason! So, for this chapter, I wanted to incorporate some of those gorgeous Mediterranean ingredients that I've used throughout the book to create something delicious to end the night. I have kept them subtle and fragrant, delicately perfumed with citrus, fruit, spice and nuts in order to create a beautiful soft finale to a wonderful meal.

I've also included two of my favorite recipes, a version of my nonna's famous tiramisu (Nonna Pia's Famous Tiramisu [page 132]), which is to die for, and an olive-oil short crust pastry crostata filled with raspberry jam (Olive Oil and Jam Crostata [page 143]). The tiramisu is so simple, which I love, because I feel as though it's known as a difficult or tedious recipe and can sometimes steer people away from making and enjoying it. The most important part is whipping the separated eggs individually in their own bowls, then it's just a matter of layering up the cake to set in the fridge. I doubt you'll find a faster or more-winning dessert or teatime treat than my crostata, which whips up at a moment's notice!

Finally, I have to suggest (read: implore) you make my Vanilla Bean and Orange Zest Semolina Custard (page 139). Patience is the main ingredient, and my goodness does it pay off! It costs pennies to make, and I often make two batches because I know I won't want to stop at one cup!

NONNA PIA'S FAMOUS TIRAMISU

Tiramisu is a traditional Venetian dessert. It is my all-time favorite. It translates to "pick me up" and does exactly that with layers of light-as-a-feather mascarpone sandwiched between coffee-and-cocoa-soaked biscuits. With my family coming from Veneto, it's something that has been made at almost every family get-together and is such an easy recipe. I really wanted to share this dessert with you because when I think of a celebration, I think of tiramisu.

COST PER SERVING: $0.75 | YIELD: 8 SERVINGS

4 eggs, separated

1 cup + 3 tbsp (250 g) superfine (caster) sugar

1½ cups (340 g) mascarpone cheese

2½ cups (625 ml) coffee

2 tbsp (11 g) Dutch-process cocoa powder, plus extra for dusting

2½ tbsp (40 ml) marsala (optional)

8½ oz (241 g) ladyfingers (savoiardi biscuits)

Add the egg yolks and sugar to the bowl of an electric mixer. Beat until the eggs turn pale and creamy. This will take a few minutes, at least. Add the mascarpone and beat until just combined and smooth and set aside.

In a separate bowl, add the egg whites and beat with clean attachments until stiff peaks form. Add half of the egg whites into the mascarpone mixture and gently fold with a spatula. Then fold in the rest of the whites.

Mix the coffee, cocoa and marsala (if using) together in a shallow container or dish. Dip the biscuits into the coffee mixture, soaking both sides, and place them in an even layer in a serving dish. (I like to use a 9 x 12-inch [23 x 29-cm] rectangular baking dish.) Spread half of the mascarpone mixture over the biscuits, then top with another layer of coffee-dipped biscuits. Spread the remaining mascarpone mixture over the biscuits and sift cocoa powder over the top. Cover and refrigerate for at least 4 hours, but preferably overnight before serving.

ITALIAN APPLE AND RICOTTA CAKE

Sweet breakfasts are very Italian—for example, a pastry or slice of freshly baked cake with an espresso at a coffee bar counter before heading off to work for the day. This cake falls somewhere between breakfast and dessert, but I figure you can have it for both! It's delicately flavored with green apple, ricotta and cinnamon, and it's also quick to put together if you have last-minute guests coming over.

COST PER SERVING: $0.35 | YIELD: 8 SERVINGS

1 egg, beaten

¼ cup (60 ml) extra virgin olive oil

½ cup + 1 tbsp (120 g) superfine (caster) sugar

⅓ cup (80 ml) milk

2 tsp (9 g) baking powder

1⅓ cups (175 g) all-purpose flour

½ tsp cinnamon

1 green apple, peeled, cored and diced

⅓ cup + 1 tbsp (100 g) ricotta cheese

Heaping ⅓ cup (45 g) slivered almonds

Honey, to drizzle

Confectioner's sugar, for dusting

Preheat the oven to 350°F (180°C). Line a 9-inch (23-cm) cake pan with parchment paper.

In a large bowl, whisk together the egg, olive oil and sugar. Add the milk and whisk again. Add the baking powder and half of the flour and mix it in slowly with the whisk before adding the rest of the flour and cinnamon. Whisk until just combined. Don't worry if there are a few lumps.

Pour the batter into the cake pan. Top the batter with the apple, small spoonfuls of ricotta, slivered almonds and a generous drizzle of honey. Bake for 30 minutes, or until an inserted skewer comes out clean.

Rest the cake for 5 minutes before carefully turning it out onto a wire rack to cool. If any almonds fall off, collect them up and put them back onto the cake. Dust with confectioners' sugar and serve warm.

SYRUPY JAM AND ALMOND CAKE

Jam is one of those items that is always in the pantry or fridge and usually saved for toast or sandwiches; however, it's a fabulously affordable ingredient that can be used to flavor biscuits, cakes and ice cream. This cake, generously spiked with strawberry jam, is also flavored with ground fennel, which complements the orange zest and strawberry wonderfully by mellowing out the sweet edge they provide. Using seasonal fruit along with nuts in desserts is something Mediterranean recipes do so well, being light and fragrant with a little goodness thrown in.

COST PER SERVING: $0.30 | YIELD: 8 SERVINGS

2 eggs

⅓ cup (80 ml) extra virgin olive oil

½ cup + 1 tbsp (120 g) superfine (caster) sugar

Zest of 1 orange

¼ cup (60 ml) milk

Just under 2 cups (230 g) flour

1 tsp ground fennel

½ cup (160 g) strawberry jam

⅓ cup (40 g) flaked almonds

Preheat the oven to 350°F (180°C). Line a 9-inch (23-cm) cake pan with parchment paper.

Add the eggs, olive oil, sugar, orange zest and milk to a large bowl. Beat together using a whisk until it's well combined. Add the flour and fennel. Mix together well, and pour the batter into the cake pan.

Top with dollops of jam, using a teaspoon to mix it a little just through the top of the cake, then sprinkle the almonds over the top. Gently press the almonds into the batter and bake for 25 minutes, or until an inserted skewer comes out clean. Cool in the pan for 5 minutes before turning out onto a wire rack to cool. Serve warm or cold.

VANILLA BEAN AND ORANGE ZEST SEMOLINA CUSTARD

This custard has the most stunning texture and flavor thanks to the understated bite semolina gives to the recipe. It's very easy to make and really only requires some patience. It reminds me of all the desserts throughout the Mediterranean, where fruit is served with various types of flan, custard or rice pudding. It's light and refreshing, making it a perfect note to end any meal on.

COST PER SERVING: $0.44 | YIELD: 4 SERVINGS

6 tbsp (80 g) superfine (caster) sugar

3 egg yolks

2½ cups (625 ml) milk

½ cup + 1½ tbsp (100 g) semolina flour

Zest of 1 orange

1 tsp (5 ml) vanilla extract

Summer fruit, for serving

Whisk together the sugar and egg yolks in a glass or ceramic bowl until pale and creamy. This takes a little muscle and about 3 to 4 minutes of whisking.

Heat a small saucepan of water over low heat, and place the bowl on top. Whisk in the milk and semolina and stir slowly for 30 minutes. (I generally sit on a stool and read or listen to music while I do this.) The custard will slowly thicken, and it will really pull together at around 25 minutes.

After 30 minutes, stir in the orange zest and vanilla, and ladle into serving cups and top with your choice of fruit. (My favorite is raspberries.) You can serve this warm or cold.

GRILLED PEARS WITH RICOTTA AND TAHINI CARAMEL

Everyone loves caramel (including me!), and this healthier version is so easy to pull together in just seconds. It's salty and sweet all at once and made with just two main ingredients that I always have on hand. Because fruit is usually eaten as a dessert throughout the Mediterranean, I thought I'd keep with that practice but grill the pears to make them soft and warm and use fresh honeyed ricotta and a drizzle of tahini caramel to top it all off.

COST PER SERVING: $1.55 | YIELD: 4 SERVINGS

FOR THE PEARS

Extra virgin olive oil, for drizzling

4 pears, cored and quartered

FOR THE RICOTTA

¾ cup + 1 tbsp (200 g) ricotta cheese

Zest of 1 lemon

2 tbsp (25 ml) honey

Pinch of cinnamon

FOR THE TAHINI CARAMEL

½ cup (130 g) hulled tahini

½ cup (125 ml) honey

Pinch of salt, plus extra as needed

1 tsp vanilla extract

To make the pears, heat a griddle pan over medium heat and add a drizzle of olive oil. Place the pears in the pan, and cook for 5 minutes, being careful to check they aren't burning. Turn them over and cook for 5 minutes. Turn them onto the final side and cook for 2 to 3 minutes, or until tender.

While the pears are cooking, combine the ricotta, lemon zest, honey and cinnamon in a bowl. Mix well.

To make the tahini caramel, place the tahini, honey, salt and vanilla in a medium bowl. Combine with a spoon. Taste it to check if it needs a little more salt. Serve the pears hot from the griddle with a dollop of ricotta and a generous drizzle of tahini caramel.

OLIVE OIL AND JAM CROSTATA

Short-crust pastries used throughout the world are traditionally made with butter, but I wanted to give this standard recipe a Mediterranean makeover by using extra virgin olive oil. And I absolutely love the result! It's much quicker to make because the dough comes together so easily with just a few kneads with the back of a spoon, and the entire recipe is incredibly prudent with just five ingredients that I have no doubt are in your pantry or fridge right now.

COST PER SERVING: $0.15 | YIELD: 6 SERVINGS

1⅓ cups (175 g) all-purpose flour

⅓ cup (80 ml) extra virgin olive oil

2 tbsp (28 g) superfine (caster) sugar, plus extra for topping

¼ cup–⅓ cup (60–80 ml) water

¾ cup (240 g) raspberry jam

Milk, for brushing

Confectioners' sugar, for dusting

Preheat the oven to 350°F (180°C).

Place the flour, oil and sugar in a large bowl. Add ¼ cup (60 ml) of water, and use a metal spoon to mix together to form a dough. I find using the back of a spoon is the best way to do this. Don't overmix the dough. When it just comes together, that's enough, and it's okay if there are white streaks through the dough. If the dough is crumbly, add the additional water, but you might not need it.

Place the dough between two sheets of parchment paper and, with a rolling pin, carefully roll it out into a rough round until the dough is about ¼ inch (6 mm) thick. The edges will be crumbly and cracked. Take off the top layer of the parchment paper and spread the jam around the middle of the dough, being careful not to spread it too close to the edges because otherwise it will spill out when it's cooking. Fold the sides in toward the middle, leaving a large area of jam exposed. If there are any cracks in the corners, gently push and knead them shut so the jam doesn't spill out.

Brush the top of the dough with milk, sprinkle confectioners' sugar over the dough and slide the dough (still on the parchment paper) onto a baking sheet. Bake for 25 to 30 minutes, or until the dough is golden. Cool and slice.

ORANGE AND HONEY COOKIE BITES

These are the most perfect little bite-size snacks to munch on with a cup of coffee. They are sweet and earthy with a touch of bitterness thanks to the orange and tahini. It's very hard to stop at one! This recipe could not be easier, using only dry pantry ingredients and one bowl. And at 20 cents per cookie, you won't need any more convincing to get started.

COST PER COOKIE: $0.20 | YIELD: 24 COOKIE BITES

¼ cup + 1 tsp (65 g) tahini

½ cup (125 ml) honey

1¼ cups (150 g) almond meal

Zest of 1 orange

½ tsp baking powder

¼ tsp salt

Pistachios, for topping

Preheat the oven to 350°F (180°C).

Place the tahini, honey, almond meal, orange zest, baking powder and salt in a large bowl. Combine well with the back of a metal spoon.

Roll small, walnut-sized equal portions of dough into balls and place them 2 inches (5 cm) apart on a parchment-lined baking sheet. (You will likely have to cook these in batches.) Gently press each ball down with two fingers and top with a pistachio.

Bake for 8 to 9 minutes until the cookies are golden. Let them cool on the baking sheet since they will be too soft to move when they're hot. Store in an airtight container.

ACKNOWLEDGMENTS

First, I would like to thank my incredible husband, Isaac, who I absolutely could not have done this without. Not only was I writing this book in isolation during a pandemic, but I was also met with huge ingredient shortages, which had Isaac running all over town at all hours trying to find flour and sugar for me. Thank you, my love, for always cheering me on, being my second set of eyes, bringing me plenty of coffee (and wine) and for just being the best. *Ti ameró per sempre amore mio.*

To my amazing family: Mum, Dad and Chelsea; Nonna and Nonno; Zia, Michelle, Dan, Olivia, Sam and Scott—thank you for teaching me how to cook, how to eat like an Italian, for always trying my ideas and for always supporting me 110 percent, even when the recipes weren't as delicious as we'd hoped. I wouldn't be where I am without you all.

To my amazing other family: Mary, Jeff and Nanna Marg—thank you for letting me feed you nonstop over the last few months and for testing out so many recipes for this book. Your constant support and encouragement means more than words can express.

To my incredible friends who jumped at the chance to test out recipes: Sarah and Damien; Simon and George; Bryce and Sarah; Nat; Ebony, Luke and Tori; Al and Nin; Taylor and Kylie—thank you! Your feedback and support have been invaluable to me, and I feel so very lucky to have you as my friends. To Camilla in London, who not only helped me remarkably with advice and counsel through many glitchy phone calls, but also ate their way through Italy with me last year. And to George, for assisting me with Photoshop and coping wonderfully with my blasé attitude toward file organization and storage.

To all of the home cooks, foodies and Instagrammers who constantly innovate, educate and excel in the craft of cooking: Thank you for your never-ending inspiration.

Finally, thank you to Page Street Publishing for giving me this opportunity. Your advice and guidance have made this book what it is, and I'll be forever grateful to you for helping my dream come true.

ABOUT THE AUTHOR

Melanie Lionello is a nutritionist, recipe developer and all-round foodie living in Melbourne, Australia, with her husband, Isaac, and her two beautiful cats, Frankie and Lulu. Her love of Mediterranean cuisine developed from her heritage and was propelled by her further studies in Turkish culinary culture.

Even though she is a university-qualified nutritionist, there's nothing she loves more than getting people into the kitchen and cooking, whether it be a simple salad or a delicious dessert. Being a dual Italian and Australian citizen, she travels each year to Italy and around the Mediterranean, where she undertakes cooking classes and workshops to learn more about the cuisine. She shares these experiences via her successful blog and Instagram, @frommylittlekitchen.

INDEX